Working Parents' Companion

OTHER TITLES IN THE SERIES

BEING PREGNANT, GIVING BIRTH
Mary Nolan

YOU AND YOUR NEW BABY
Anna McGrail

BREASTFEEDING YOUR BABY
Jane Moody, Jane Britten and Karen Hogg

Working Parents' Companion

Teresa Wilson

A
NATIONAL CHILDBIRTH TRUST GUIDE

Published by National Childbirth Trust Publishing
in collaboration with Thorsons

Thorsons
An Imprint of HarperCollins*Publishers*

Picture Acknowledgements
The publishers would like to thank the following for their permission to
reproduce photographs: Zefa/Ronnie Kaufman: Cover;
Michael Bassett: ppxii, 30, 88, 100, 122; Eddie Lawrence: p20;
Julian Cotton Photo Library: p46; The Image Bank/M. Regine: p58;
The Image Bank/Romilly Lockyer: p72; Graham Bell: p130; Egnell Ameda: p144.

Illustrations:
Mike Edwards, Pete Welford, Jo Dennis.

Design by Tim McPhee.

Production in association with
Book Production Consultants plc,
25–27 High Street, Chesterton, Cambridge CB4 1ND, UK.

Printed by Hillman Printers (Frome) Ltd,
Frome, Somerset.

Published by National Childbirth Trust Publishing,
25-27 High Street, Chesterton, Cambridge CB4 1ND, UK.

in collaboration with Thorsons
An Imprint of HarperCollins *Publishers*
77–85 Fulham Palace Road, Hammersmith, London W6 8JB.

© 1996 NCT Publishing

First published as *Work and Home* 1996
This edition 1998

A CIP catalogue record for this book is available from the British Library.

ISBN 0 7225 3638 0

Contents

ABOUT THE AUTHOR   vii

PUBLISHER'S NOTE   ix

ACKNOWLEDGEMENTS   ix

INTRODUCTION   xi

CHAPTER ONE – WHY DO
WOMEN RETURN TO WORK?   1
The wider picture   1
Reasons for returning   3
Work and lifestyles   12

CHAPTER TWO – TALKING
ABOUT FEELINGS   21
Personal experiences   21

CHAPTER THREE – ACHIEVING
A BALANCE BETWEEN WORK
AND HOME   31
How your working life may change   31
The obstacles to achieving a balance   32
Solutions   40

CHAPTER FOUR – TIME OFF –
LIFE AS A FAMILY   47
Shared parenting   47
Unexpected events   51
Changing priorities   51
Partnership pressures   52

Single parenting and support   54
Family activities   55

CHAPTER FIVE – THINKING
ABOUT CHILDCARE   59
Initial thoughts   59
Childcare choices   60
Difficult times   65
Questions to ask yourself   66
Selecting and interviewing   68
Contracts   70

CHAPTER SIX –
CHILDMINDERS   73
Childminders   73
The advantages   74
The disadvantages   77
From the childminder's point of view 81
Finding a childminder   87

CHAPTER SEVEN – NURSERIES
AND CRECHES   89
The nursery and the workplace crèche 89
Advantages of the nursery or crèche   89
Disadvantages of the nursery or crèche 92
Choices and children   93
The view from the nursery   96
What should you look for when
choosing a nursery?   98
Finding a nursery   99

CHAPTER EIGHT – NANNIES   101
A nanny   101
Advantages of the live-in nanny   102
Disadvantages of the live-in nanny   105
Daily nanny   107
The nanny from Hell   108
Nanny share   110
Finding a nanny   113
Telephone interviewing   113
Interviewing face to face   115
Contracts   118

CHAPTER NINE – AU PAIRS AND
OTHER SUPPORT   123
Maternity nurses   123
Mother's help   124
Au pair/au pair plus   125
Advantages of the au pair scheme   126
Disadvantages of the au pair scheme 127
Finding an au pair   129

CHAPTER TEN – INFORMAL
CHILDCARE AND AFTER –
SCHOOL OPTIONS   131
Changing needs   131
School days   137
The school holidays   139

CHAPTER ELEVEN – BREAST-
FEEDING AND WORKING   145
Do you have to give up?   146
Reasons to continue breastfeeding   147
Breastfeeding – how it works   148
Night-time with your baby   151
Expressing milk   152
Babies and bottles   162
Breastfeeding and the working
mother   166
Problems with breastfeeding and
working   169
Worth the extra effort   169

CONCLUSION   170
Finding the balance   170

DIRECTORY   172

FURTHER READING   176

INDEX   177

About the author

TERESA WILSON has tried all ways and combinations of working and running a family. She has been a full-time, stay-at-home mother, worked part time and full time. Over the years she has come to the conclusion that each has its own advantages and disadvantages. She thinks it is important to accept that your life will be constantly changing once you have had children and that different ways of working will suit different stages in your life as a family.

She has three children, aged 15, 5 and 2. She is a breastfeeding counsellor and trainee postnatal discussion leader for the NCT, and books editor for *New Generation*, the journal of the NCT.

Publisher's note

ALL COMMENTS and personal accounts were given to us in confidence, so out of respect for our contributors' privacy we have changed all the names.

We have endeavoured where possible to reproduce quotations verbatim, but where editing has been applied, the integrity of the quotation has been maintained.

Acknowledgements

ARE NUMEROUS. First, a large thank-you to my family, who tolerated my working the most anti-social hours for six months and cleared up the mess after me. Particular thanks are due to my husband, Rick, who spent many solitary evenings, and acted as a single parent most weekends, and my dear mum, Pat, who did everything she could to ease the load, so I could get on. Anyone who wonders if they can work from home with children about – take it from me – you can't! So without their unstinting support, this book would not have got written.

Thanks also to Vanessa Von Pralitz and Alison Howarth-Jarrett who supported me with childcare at short notice and to Jenny Jolliffe for reading and checking the manuscript.

Many thanks also to the working parents who gave up their precious time to talk to me. I know it wasn't always easy to give it, but they wanted to talk about the pleasures and pitfalls of their lifestyle and pass on things they wish they had known in retrospect.

Finally, thank you to my editor, Daphne Metland, whose firm direction supported and motivated me along the way.

This book is dedicated to my children: Mat, Sean and Alex.

THE NATIONAL CHILDBIRTH TRUST (NCT) offers information and support in pregnancy, childbirth and early parenthood. We aim to give every parent the chance to make informed choices. We try to make sure that our services, activities and membership are fully accessible to everyone. Donations to support our work are welcome.

Introduction

THIS BOOK AIMS to give a broad overview of how women are combining bringing up their children and working.

There are important decisions to be made: whether to go back at all, whether to choose a new way of working and what sort of childcare will be most suitable. Your decision will also depend on how old your child is when you return. Then, when you think life is getting easier, along comes school to throw a spanner in the works. How do you cope with all those holidays?

A working family also brings into sharper relief the pressures of work and the lack of time available for leisure pursuits and enjoying the children. For couples, there may be discussions on how best to work together and share the parenting role, and for single parents, there are other issues of sole parenting and support.

One of the most common truisms is that there is never enough time for everything. If you have a whole day at work you still have to do the chores for that day, and give your child your full attention.

Most parents successfully combine working and parenting, but it can be stressful and it can be very tiring. On a good day it can give you a sense of satisfaction, a sense of achievement and a new dimension to life. The balance between your commitment to a job and your commitment to the family can be hard to maintain, and there may be times when you need to place a greater emphasis on one or the other.

I spoke to many working parents whilst researching this book. I hope their views and experiences are a fair reflection of society in general and the questions raised about being a working parent.

I have aimed to reflect the many different ways of working which now exist and the wide choice of childcare that is available. One important observation that all those I spoke to shared was: the decision to return to work, whatever your circumstances, is never an easy one to make.

CHAPTER <u>*one*</u> *Why do women return to work?*

THE WIDER PICTURE

UNTIL RECENTLY the issue of whether to return to work or not after starting a family was much more clear cut. Families were started earlier, often soon after marriage and for many women the question of work was not even raised. For others, starting a family implied that you intended to opt out of the working environment, at least until your children had left home, then maybe you'd start to do voluntary work or take on a part-time, non-demanding job. For some women there was no question of having children, because it would interfere with their career.

Viewed from the 1990s, when choice is paramount, this situation appears restrictive, inflexible and not at all family-friendly. For women today, combining a working life with having a family is possible and is gradually becoming easier with a slow, but steady, increase in the provision of childcare. No longer do women have to choose between returning to work full time or risk losing their jobs; employers, encouraged by new legislation, have to show a flexible attitude to their female employees.

Guilt

IT'S WORTH getting this word out in the open early on. As we look at why women want to return to work, there is a cloud gathering which spells out the word 'guilt'. Some women are still told that they ought to feel guilty about leaving their child to pursue their career. Others spend some time feeling guilty about not feeling guilty when they leave their child – again, it is a personal issue. There is no doubt that many women do suffer from strong feelings of guilt about returning to work. Some come to terms with it because they know their option

YOUR MATERNITY RIGHTS

Working pregnant women are entitled to certain legal rights to protect your health and your job, and in many cases to some financial help when you have your baby. It's worth checking these, as they are quite complex and the law changes from time to time. The main benefits are:

Statutory Maternity Leave

Every woman is entitled to 14 weeks' maternity leave if she is in work while she is pregnant. This is regardless of whether the post is full or part time. If you have been working for your employer for two years by the end of the 12th week before the baby is due you are able to take extended maternity absence of 29 weeks from birth.

Statutory Maternity Pay (SMP)

You are entitled to receive this for 18 weeks from the day you stop work, but the actual amounts may vary according to your existing salary. You must have worked for the same employer for at least 26 weeks by the end of the qualifying week (the week 15 weeks before the beginning of the week in which the baby is due) and you must still be in your job in this 15th week and you must be earning £58 a week or more on average.

Maternity Allowance

If you are not entitled to SMP you may be able to claim Maternity Allowance. Your midwife will be able to supply you with the appropriate form, or contact your local Benefits Agency. For more information on Maternity Rights send for a leaflet from Maternity Alliance.

was a financial necessity. Others feel guilty until they know that their child is happy in their new environment.

Your rights

MATERNITY RIGHTS have improved for all women, and as more and more women exercise these rights and push legislation to its limits, the situation can only improve. For details of your entitlements contact your Social Security Department and Employment Services who can provide you with numerous leaflets and publications.

The Maternity Alliance can supply you with useful leaflets (see address in Directory).

Although conditions are improving in the United Kingdom, there is still a long way to go before we reach standards available in Sweden.

SWEDISH RIGHTS

Since the early 1970s Sweden has had a state policy and benefits aimed at helping parents, not just mothers, to remain at work while caring for children. In Sweden employment entitlements include:

● Pregnancy leave of 50 days
● Paternity leave of ten days
● Parental leave (to care for young children or babies) of 12 months per child
● Leave of 90 days per year per child under 12 to care for them if sick or if their minder is sick.

All these are paid state benefits at 80–100% of earnings.

REASONS FOR RETURNING

Isolation of motherhood

ONE OF the most difficult issues that mothers have to face, when they have their first child, is the isolation.

Very often they have been working in a different neighbourhood to their home, so they don't know the neighbours very well. People who go off for the day to work and those who stay at home lead different lives, and it takes a while to adjust. A working woman will also generally have been in control of her life – able to make spontaneous decisions and act upon them. The arrival of a child frustrates this spontaneity for a while, and there is no one to turn to at this stage. No wonder people yearn to go back to the warmth and friendliness of a working life.

Pat talks about her experience: *'Sam was born in November, the clocks had gone back. It was dark by four. I can remember that horrible time between four and six, waiting for Simon to come home. I was desperate for him to come through the door, so I could hand over to him. Because I had worked in London, I didn't know many people locally, particularly with babies – you don't have time, and it takes a while to build up contacts. Before you have children, your network is in the office.*

I was also very cautious about going out with the pram in the snow and ice – all this made me feel very cooped up.'

Louise felt the same way about this: *'After your first baby, there is no social sphere. It's that endless day, and you're not used to having an endless day. There's only so much shopping that you can do.'*

IF YOU do feel isolated, what steps can you take?

REASONS

- Need to contribute financially to the household
- Need to support the family financially: redundancy
- Emotional need to work
- Intellectual need to work
- Single parenthood
- Planning for the future – pensions and security
- Keeping a hand in
- Maintaining an established career
- Benefiting your children
- A sense of your own value
- Improved childcare provision
- Childhood influences.

HOW TO MEET OTHER PEOPLE

- Your local NCT group
- Your baby clinic
- Postnatal discussion and/or exercise classes
- Aquanatal classes
- Local women's group.

It certainly can take a long time to build up a new set of contacts and friends when you have a baby. The NCT is a good medium to use for this – they have neighbourhood support networks, postnatal supporters and lots of people even find themselves going along to coffee mornings, and not only that, but they meet other people who also never thought they'd be seen dead at a coffee morning.

Even though you may be returning to work in three months' time, it can be well worth getting to know local people with babies and young children.

Sometimes when you are at work, you can feel isolated from what your baby is doing during the week and who he is meeting, so it's nice to get to meet up with these people and their children at weekends.

A need for more than just babies . . .

AMY HAD the same views as her husband: *'We wanted to have an equal, sharing partnership. Neither of us liked the idea of me being solely preoccupied by household issues. My first baby was fourteen months old when my second baby was born. I'm sure I would have found having two babies for company all day very frustrating.'*

SOME WOMEN feel that being at home with the baby would not stretch them enough, and they become better mothers for being intellectually satisfied.

Beth feels like this. She is the disabled mother of five children, but feels strongly that both she, and the children, gain by her working: *'If I am not working, then I start mentally climbing walls. I am just an intellectual person – I need the stimulation.'*

Do the children benefit?

THE IDEA that the added stimulus of work gives one more to give back to the children is quite a common feeling.

'I think I personally would be a worse mother being at home all day. If you are not with the children all the time, you enjoy seeing them all the more when you do see them, and enjoy doing things with them, too.'

'I know that my kids like me working. I am a better mother if I am fulfilled. It also means I can use my work as a tool when spending time with my children. For example, I've just learnt British Sign Language – I can talk to my children about it, share it. As a teacher, we all enjoy doing homework together. It becomes a positive experience.'

Kerrie also felt a need to use her brain in the work environment too: *'I didn't know many people locally before having Jo, so everyone we know here we know as a result of Jo, and the thing we have in common is the children, and that's what we talk about, which is fine. But I also really appreciate the opportunity to talk to other people about other things. I like working with people. I like managing people, so that's what I value work for: the opportunity to use my brain.'*

Future security

TODAY, MANY women want to be in control of their own destiny. With the divorce rate high, there is a greater need to protect oneself from a possible financial disaster.

Even without taking a career break, women can be at a disadvantage when it comes to pension payments: women live longer, so they have to put more into their pension scheme to get the same amount out, because it has got to last those extra few years.

During a career break you can't pay into a pension scheme, because payments have to be made from earned income, in order for them to benefit from tax relief. This means that women who are looking at their own financial security are unlikely to want to give up five or so years of payments when they will need more to benefit from in later years. There are ways round the problem, like taking out a Personal Equity Plan (PEP) during a career break, assuming you have the cash flow when you aren't working.

Sue learned from the experience of her parents' separation that nothing is set in tablets of stone: *'My parents split up and that has made me feel that I need to know that I can cope if the unexpected happens. It's important to me to have that sense of security. I need a degree of independence. Although I'm together with Alan, I need to know that if something happened, I could cope.'*

THIS SENSE of responsibility grows with the arrival of children for whom one must provide, and that is no longer seen as solely the male domain.

It's not only divorce that is being considered here, but sometimes partners die young. In other words, the unspeakable does happen, and some women are making moves to protect themselves against at least one ramification of it.

Keeping a hand in

MANY ASPECTS of work life change rapidly now. In order to remain employable, it is necessary to keep abreast of progress in any particular field.

Ria, for example, is a scientist: *'Things move very fast. I have to stay involved with the profession in order to move with it.'*

CAREER BREAKS are available with some companies, but it's necessary, generally, to go in at least for two weeks every year, to keep up and update work skills. This is particularly the case if computers are in any way involved in your working life.

Sue is an accountant: *'In this career you would be out of date if you left it for a couple of years. Also, I'm not a very confident person – I can't bluff my way into a job, so I need to know that my knowledge is thorough.'*

BEING SEEN to be there, rather than the message filtering through that you are doing mothering now, can make a difference to your own sense of self-esteem at work. It can seem easy to feel written off if you're not around the office for a few months. And what happens when you come back? There's no doubt that it must be harder to find the right niche if you have to push your way back into the market a couple of years on with rusty skills.

There are other reasons too why you might need to stay where you are. Frances is blind. *'If I was sighted, I wouldn't feel the need to keep the job open in the same way, but it was much more difficult for me to get a job when I left university than any of my contemporaries. I can't give it up now.'*

Maintaining a career and way of life

HAVING A BABY after a career has become established means that there is more to lose by giving up work and staying at home with the baby.

As Harriet says, *'I worked so hard to get where I am now, I didn't want to give all that up.'*

FOR SOME, too, there is the belief that you don't have to give anything up – the idea of Superwoman still prevails. Very often, childless couples tend to socialise with other childless friends. That, together with greater mobility of families means that there are fewer occasions where a childless or pregnant woman is likely to see the reality of how much time and effort a baby takes up. There is no reason to think that a baby will change things, particularly the way that you feel.

Pat says that: *'You think life is going to be the same. You have no idea how it will really change your life. If you have a career you don't want to lose out.'*

A financial need

THERE ARE MANY, many people who have to go back to work, not because they want to, but because living is very expensive now. Carolyn had to return to work earlier than she had anticipated because she and her husband could no longer manage without the extra salary: *'I wanted to get by until Tom was at school, but he was still three when business problems meant that not only was money tight, but we were getting into debt too. Going back to work was the only available option and I had to do it. But the funny thing is that, now I've started work, I find I need it, it's reawakened my brain, and I wouldn't be happy walking to school and back any more. Part of it I miss . . . to chat . . . but I wouldn't want to stop work.'*

UNFORTUNATELY redundancy is not as unusual as it used to be – it is a fact of many people's lives. Whereas some years ago it was possible to believe that you had a job for life, unless disaster befell you or the company, today redundancies are all too common.

For Joan, her husband's redundancy meant, amongst other things, a lot of resentment: *'When Peter lost his job my feeling was, and still is, that it isn't fair. We waited a long time before having our family, so that we would be financially secure, and I could stay at home and look after them. Now I have to work, just to keep the bills paid, not even to pay for the luxuries in life.'*

Childhood influences

OUR OWN mothers are generally our first role model, and what they did when we were children can have a strong influence on what we do ourselves. *'Since my mother worked, we had nannies: there were four of us – all girls. We had a very happy childhood and the nannies became part of the family. In fact, the last one is still living with my parents. I've followed in my mother's footsteps and my children are looked after by a live-in nanny.'*

On the other hand, some daughters prefer to opt for the complete opposite of what their mother did, like Sue: *'My mother was always there with me. She never left me to play. As a result of this I was a very clingy child, and I think a lot of that was due to not mixing very much, and being with my mother most of the time. I wouldn't want my daughter to be as dependent upon me as I was on my mother so I've gone back to work part time.'*

Vanessa's own childhood had the opposite effect on her: *'I was born in Africa, and had quite a colonial upbringing. We had servants, including a nanny, but when I was seven and my sister was five, we were sent to boarding school in England. The reason given was that there was no decent education where we were. I hated it. I was continually writing to my parents to take me away. We only saw our parents once a year, during the summer holidays. Our grandparents were over in England so we weren't completely isolated, but that didn't help much.'* Vanessa feels that this has a lot to do with why she became a childminder, rather than going back to work and organising childcare for her own children.

Lindsay also felt that she wanted to work, but also to be with her children, so she took on work that she could do from home: *'My priority is to be there for my children, as my mother had been throughout my childhood. But I also thought it was important for me to use my brain. Working from home seems to provide the answer so far.'*

But Kerrie found her parents a very useful role model of a couple who successfully combined working with bringing up children. *'Having working parents makes you aware that you can have two working adults in the family – and things work.'*

Single parenthood

BEING A SINGLE parent is likely to restrict the number of choices you
have available to you, unless you are financially secure. A household
that has two people earning in it can look at the most cost-efficient
way of bringing up a family. If there is only you, there is only one
salary. You may need to be looking at the balance between income
and outgoing payments for childcare, travelling and so on. It may be
that, depending on your salary, it is not financially viable to work. By
the time all the necessary payments have been made for childcare, you
may be worse off than you would be if you were eligible for benefits.

One aspect of single parenting that could make a parent want to get
back out to work is the greater sense of isolation a single mother may

experience. If you are at home with the children, and your partner comes home, you can hand over responsibility to him/her for a while, at least, and re-humanise yourself. You also have someone to let off steam to, someone who can listen to you talking in the minutest detail about the colour of the baby's dirty nappies that day, or the number of gurgles that she gave, or how you are absolutely sure that she's starting to smile at you now.

If you are parenting on your own, you don't have that luxury. It's down to you to notice these things. Doubtless there are other people that you can talk to about your baby's development, but not many on the same, regular basis. But whilst babies are very lovable and you may want to talk about them, single parenting can be relentless with little opportunity to be an adult with another person.

Having a job to go to could, therefore, be more important if you are not sharing your life with another adult. It means that you can function on two levels, rather than being constantly involved with children. It gives a social outlet that makes you an autonomous being, and gives a sense of independence.

It is also worth looking at from the point of view of the children. It may be that the children benefit from having different adults looking after them during the day, so they can learn more about socialising and relating to other people apart from their parent.

A sense of your own value

PARENTHOOD CAN change your perception of the world and where you fit in: in some quarters you are accepted and respected, in others you may notice reservation, even resentment and envy.

When you are deciding whether to return to work or not you may feel weighed down by decisions and legislation; it doesn't help to have to deal with an unsupportive employer. You may begin to feel that there is little chance of being able to get what you want.

Alex is a marketing director, but when she became pregnant for the first time, she was a marketing manager: *'It is very important to negotiate for what you want. When you are in the job, you are in a stronger position. Of course you will be told that they don't do that here, but there's a first time for everything.*

I think that women often don't value themselves enough. They think that they have to take what is offered because they are lucky to have a job. But if they are doing that job well, the company won't want to lose them. They have spent money training them and they are a valuable asset to the company. It's worth hanging on to this when you ask for conditions that suit your situation.'

THERE ARE so many more mothers returning to work now that it should be possible to find jobs that are family-friendly. From the interviews that have been done for this book, it seems clear that most working mothers, particularly part-timers, work harder than before in order to justify having shortened hours. So most companies won't lose anything, but will gain loyal members of their workforce.

WORK AND LIFESTYLES

WOMEN ARE learning to adapt work to suit their lifestyle, rather than sacrificing all their personal goals for 'the job'. Children and their needs are being given priority, but not to the detriment of their mother's own need to return to work. The choice is wide: part time, temporary jobs, freelance or self-employed, role reversal, temporary contracts for jobs different to those they trained for, flexitime, job-shares, a career break and, of course, full time.

Much of this flexibility has been made possible through the increasing use of technology; companies are beginning to realise that valuable employees in whom they have invested time and money do not have to be wasted or lost to another company. There is evidence to suggest that many working mothers are now being employed in a home office. Companies provide them with a computer, phone and fax in their own homes and may expect a personal visit once a week or not at all. The advantages for the employers, once the home office has been set up, include a decrease in overheads and an increase in flexibility. For the employees, this type of

---

1994 International Year of the Family

Parliamentary Hearings included statements on Families and Work. One of the most significant changes discussed was the decline over the last 20 years of the sole, male breadwinner family, and the rise of the dual earner family. In 1973, in 43% of families, both partners worked, compared to 60% in 1992. However, it was found that very few women returned to work full time, only 14% in 1992, and of those women most were professionals or non-manual workers.

working style can ease many practical and financial pressures: shorter journeys to pick up and drop off children; flexibility in working hours if necessary; fewer smart office clothes to buy. However, one of the disadvantages could be the loss of social contact which only an office can provide.

Returning to work full time

WHILST THIS might seem a tiring option, it is a feasible choice that many women opt for. There are some workplace nurseries springing up to cater for the growing demand of parents.

One of the problems of working full time is that you often feel that you are not allowed to acknowledge having a family – you have to deny this bit of yourself in order to get on.

A career change

SYLVETTE THOUGHT that when she returned to work, she would change from being a computer consultant to doing something more 'socially beneficial'. She enrolled on a course in counselling. Emma was eight months when she started: *'Studying was compatible with having a baby, but only just. I went for the option of the full-time course, to get it done in one year, and I thought I could get away with not using the library during study days, but it was very hard for a while.*

There was a lot of work during the second term. I managed okay during the first term, because Rob had Emma on Saturday mornings, which gave me some time, although it was hard to be in the same house if she was crying downstairs. In the second term I needed more time, so it got harder.

Before we had Emma, the idea that our roles would be shared was there, but somehow it ended up with me taking the brunt of responsibility. When I started at college things balanced out a bit, because Rob had to do more: I couldn't do the course and do everything else, so he had to get more involved.

The other side of that were the difficulties that Rob faced. I had to work at weekends. I was just too tired to work in the evenings.'

DEBBIE HAS TWO daughters, aged eight and six. She works as a volunteer at her daughters' school, helping out with reading and sewing in the classrooms. She also works as a cleaner, in homes and occasionally at a local school: '*I like to earn some money to pay for the extras in our life, for example, to get nice things for the girls. Also, if I didn't do this, we wouldn't have money to go out. My money is what we save for that sort of thing – my husband's is for the day-to-day running of the home.*

I find my work exhausting, because you really have to have some energy when the girls come in from school, as I like to be involved with them then. It does make me feel that I'm too tired to cook.

If you work, your whole day is extended, because you have to do your own housework at the end of the day, like getting their school stuff ready, and dusting and polishing.

But I don't want to go back to any other sort of work until the girls are in their teens. I have got qualifications but if I worked full time in a more responsible job I wouldn't be able to give my children the time they need. If I got a childminder I'd have to give all my money to them.'

Karen is married to Robin. They have two children, aged five and two: '*Before I had the children, I worked as a co-ordinator in a printing firm. I wouldn't have left but for the fact I was pregnant. They did offer me an option of going back, but I didn't know of anyone who could look after my son, and I wouldn't leave him with a stranger. I know I wouldn't be able to relax if he was with a minder. My mum does live locally but she's too old to take on a young child.*

Although I was happy to give up work, I have to admit that when you stop, you can become brain dead. That's what being with children all the time can do to you. After my second child, John, was born, I got a pub job five minutes down the road. It was pure and simple, and I really did enjoy it, although the late nights were shattering, particularly as John wasn't a great sleeper. I found it was a great release: it was busy and we had a laugh. I did it for three or four nights a week, and at the time, Robin was at college the other two nights a week and football training on another. We didn't see very much of each other, but we knew it wasn't permanent, and it paid for my driving lessons, so it didn't bother us.

In the end it all got a bit too much because John's sleeping was so broken, and the landlord wasn't flexible about how many nights I could do – it was all or nothing.'

Career break

FOR SOME, like Nina, the answer is a career break: *'I was working in marketing and product development, I was five weeks' pregnant, and offered a promotion. I was in a dilemma, but I took the job, having told my employers that I was pregnant. I tried to be as co-operative as I could. But the more I thought about it, the more I wanted to go for a career break, which I applied for, and was offered. I felt that I got it because I had skills that they valued, but also because I was straight with them in my early pregnancy.*

The career break in my company could be for up to five years. Anyone could apply, not just women and a contract would guarantee a job of the same status and salary as before – but not the same job, necessarily.

If I hadn't been offered the break, I would have given up the job, so it's been very good for me, and gives me a fall-back option if, for example, something happened to my husband, like an accident or redundancy.

I think it's very important to be at home with my children, and I'm not sure if this break will be long enough for me. I like to give them security and routine and I don't want anyone else to bring them up. Five years is okay if you are only having one child, but if you have two or three, it's not enough if you want to wait till the youngest is at school.

My contract stipulates that I go in for a fortnight every year, to keep up with training and so on, and I thoroughly enjoy it when I go. On the last visit I made, I was asked to take on some project work at home – my instinct was to say yes, but in the end I decided against it, as I didn't want to have another focus of attention.'

Part-time work

THIS COVERS a multitude of options, from one day a week to 30 hours a week. If you are in a position to do it then it is a valuable option.

Some people appreciate the status of part-time work, which raises their self-esteem, whilst also giving them the time to get to know people locally, and to enjoy being with the children.

The trouble with part-time work is getting interesting jobs, though in some areas it is possible to return to a previous job at the same grade. For too long, part-time work has been the domain of the female, low-paid worker.

Many are told that their jobs can't be done part time, because they have to be seen to be there. There is dispute about this. Laura says: *'Communication is very important. If you are not there, people need to know when you are available. It's a question of delivering information.'*

Working from home

THE DREAM is there: the ideal solution, working away in between breastfeeding the baby and playing with their toys with them. But it isn't always as simple as that.

Zoe relates: *'Everyone who has children and who has tried to work from home will come up with similar, and often seemingly apocryphal stories, except, given the constant nature of children and the intractable nature of working from home, they probably are all true.*

I really was on the phone to a High Official who was giving me his comments on the latest draft of a contract I'd been working on for the Home Office when my two-year-old son entered, shouting his demand for assistance with his overall buckles.

"Go away", I hissed, flinging maternal concern to the winds in the quest to preserve my professional image.

"But I need to do a poo", he wailed.

"Then wait just a minute." At this point I tried to push him under the desk, if memory serves.

"But..."

"Wait!"

"But it's coming out!"

"Is there a problem?" said the Home Office.

"None at all," I said. "Afternoon play on Radio Four."

Since then I have weathered: my daughter's lost dummy falling out of a folder during a meeting, which might have been successfully ignored, had I not fallen on it with delight, crying, "At last, a peaceful night!"; expressed breast milk leaking from the bottle in my briefcase onto a computer disk, also in my briefcase, the sticky disk then blocked up my disk drive with coagulated expressed milk, which not only defeated the computer repair men but which also smelled absolutely disgusting . . . for weeks and weeks; guilt – endless and destructive.'

Ria is working on a part-time contract from home. Her brief is that she works 850 hours over a year, so she can arrange her hours as she wishes, which fits in with her two children. The only stipulation is that she goes into the office for four days a month, which she enjoys. *'I don't feel so valued, working from home. Other people know I'm back if I go in once a week.'* Because she has an annual target of hours to meet, she can arrange her schedule so that she doesn't work during school holidays. *'The main disadvantage of it is I feel so guilty if I stop for a break. It's the sort of thing you don't think twice about when you're in an office.'*

Flexitime

THIS IS something that is becoming more popular. It worked for Alex, because although she has to work her 37 hours a week, she can do it when she likes: *'I feel that this is a good compromise. I can get up one or two mornings a week and go into work at about 6.30am. This means I'm home for the children at tea and bed times, which is very important to me.'*

Self-employed

SOME PARENTS want to work again very badly, maybe for extra income, or perhaps because they want to get more out of life than caring for the children. But they are not prepared to leave the children, so they make other arrangements.

Lindsay wanted to work, but wanted to look after her family: *'I've always made clothes for family and friends, so it was a natural extension of this to start selling them. I used a party plan system, inviting friends or holding NCT coffee mornings where my clothes were for sale. I would take the orders and make up the clothes in the evenings.*

When my second son was born, getting everything organised became more problematic. Spare time was reduced because of the baby, and as the orders took longer to make up, so I felt guiltier about keeping people waiting. So I cut right back again, sticking just to family and friends. Although the financial side suffered, this is one of the things that I like about this type of work: you can do it at your own pace.

It's important for me to be close to my children while they are young. When we decided to have children, we mutually agreed that I would care for them during those early years.

As Greg has got older, I've started selling children's books, and I can take the children along with me too. One thing I miss is the companionship of colleagues and the social life of work, but I have a supervisor who I can talk things through with, and that helps.'

Phoebe worked in a high-pressure, stressful, marketing and communications company for several years, then she discovered she was pregnant: *'During my pregnancy and my maternity absence I worked hard to establish freelance contacts, with a view to becoming a self-employed editor instead of returning to being employed part time. A week before the date I was due to return I took the plunge.*

I had arranged a local childminder for my six-month-old baby, Rose, for two days a week. This gave me two clear days to work and the rest of the week to enjoy being a mother. The disadvantages soon made themselves known, but did not deter my plans: when Rose was ill, the childminder could not take her, so I lost my two days and had to work at other times to meet my deadlines, including weekends.'

BEING SELF-EMPLOYED can give you flexibility, a sense of freedom and control, but it can also be insecure, lonely and intrusive on your family life. But with advances in technology it will become an increasingly popular work option for many women.

Role reversal

FOR SOME PARENTS this seems to be the obvious solution to childcare problems, and it may well suit their own personal views on working and not working.

Lois and Nick found this change was rather forced upon them by circumstances: Nick's job was very stressful; he had a lot of travelling to do. One day he had a breakdown; he went home and has never been back. The question was, what to do afterwards. His wife Lois did freelance consultancy work and they decided to try role reversal:

'I didn't know whether I'd have the patience,' says Nick, *'but I've learnt that as long as you can get through the day, not expecting to achieve too much, you're doing okay.'*

Their two children are now two and a half and three months. When Lois works away, they all go with her, when possible, and Nick is there holding the baby to pass over to her at lunchtimes for breast-feeding: *'It's working for me. I don't have to commute, I'm seeing more of the children, I have more time to spare and my life is less stressful. I'm happy in this role. I imagined there would be more time, but there isn't much left over for dusting and hoovering.'*

Lois is delighted that Nick is looking after the children. *'I think other men who hear about him think: you lucky so and so. The more we thought about it, the more it seemed like a good idea. He'd always wanted to stop work early.'* Other people, however, have found it more difficult to accept this role reversal, including their parents. But both Nick and Lois wouldn't change it again: *'I am surprised how easy it is to look after a baby – it's given me new knowledge'*, says Nick.

And Lois: *'I could miss them, but I relish the time without them – I paint my toenails.'*

CHAPTER *two* *Talking about feelings*

WHATEVER THE REASON for returning to work and whatever work-style is chosen, there is no doubt that it is a period in parents' lives when very strong emotions are aroused. All these mixed emotions have an impact on self-esteem, relationships and future plans – an impact that can be negative, or positive, or both.

Listening to other parents' experiences may help – it will show that there are no rights and wrongs: parenthood is unique to each parent.

PERSONAL EXPERIENCES

SUE HAD a very difficult birth with her first child and the bonding process wasn't helped by Abi's 'clicky hip', which was in plaster. *'My mother came to help me when Abi was born, which was tremendous, but inevitably the time came when my husband went back to work and my mother went home. I was very lonely and very depressed. We were quite new to the area, so I had no contacts, no neighbours I knew, no NCT. I got so depressed that at one stage I took to the bottle. One afternoon John came home early and I'd already been at the sherry bottle. That's how bad it had got. My experience of being a mother was so awful that I couldn't wait to get back to work. I couldn't stand the isolation – I had been independent before my marriage at the age of 30 and by the age of 31 I had gone from independence to motherhood in a backwater.*

So I went back to work full time as a teacher as soon as I could, and it was such a relief. The carer gave me every confidence, she was very calm, and the school was close by. I really felt that it was better for Abi too. And of course being a teacher I could pick her up at about 3.30pm. I was pleased to go back, but then John's job moved him to London. The good news about that was that we were nearer to John's parents, but I had other news too: I had to give up my job and the next bombshell, which was confirmed before Abi's first birthday, was that I was pregnant.

When Helen was born it was a different experience to the first one. Because of an anal fissure I had to be very careful of pushing, and I had to have an episiotomy. But apart from that there was no intervention: no forceps, the baby was fine, so we were able to get closer and the feeding went well. Those first six weeks were so different. But it made me see how hard it had been for me last time – I had been in agony compared to this. I realised what I had been through with Abi.

I fed Helen for eight months and although everything was easier I was bored at home with a toddler and a baby, so I found some work teaching part time. Abi went to nursery in the mornings and either my mother or John's mother would have the two of them in the afternoons. Later on Helen went to a childminder. I used to cry when I left her but she never did. My mother thought that what I was doing was wrong – she'd say, "I hope you won't regret this in later life". I knew I had to do it for my own sanity. I'd gone into teaching late and I wanted to get back into it.

It was also important for me to be back at work because of my relationship with my husband. We had met, got engaged very quickly, and before we knew it, I was up to my eyes in children. I was getting little sleep, I was ratty and I had low self-esteem at the time – we didn't communicate well during those years, but I felt it was important not to be just a housewife. John was younger than me, and all of a sudden he had a wife, a mortgage, kids, the lot. My mother used to say: "You must make an effort. No husband wants to come home to an exhausted wife and no dinner". But I had to feed the children, and bath them and put them to bed. To me married life was all bringing up children.

I think that because we were having such a rough time, it was important to me to keep up the identity I got with the job, so I wasn't just a mother. I went back to full-time as soon as I could, and our marriage has lasted.'

Elizabeth found that being a single parent can be restrictive if you want to work: *'My parents are based in the Middle East, where I had lived since I was four. I went over to stay with them when Sian was coming up to two years old, and I was offered a job in a nursery. There is a strong emphasis over there that you earn a job because of your ability to do it, not just your qualifications. I had worked with handicapped children, and had been a nanny, as well as having my own little girl, and I jumped at the chance of this job.*

Both of my parents were working over there, so I got a nursery place for Sian too, in a different room to the one I was in. She settled in brilliantly so

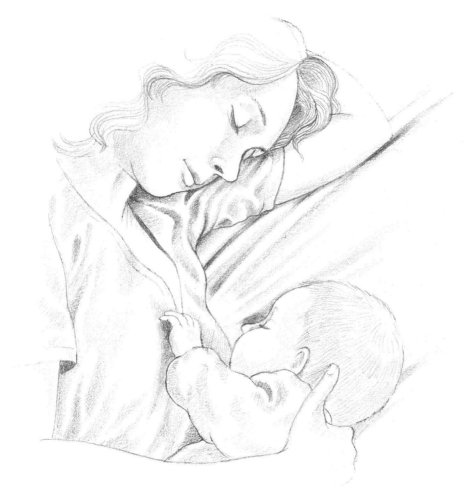

it wasn't a difficult decision to take the job. I wanted to do it partly to get away from Sian for a little while. Don't get me wrong, but sometimes it's good to have a break, however much you love your child.

I'm not on my own through choice, but I have to say that whilst you miss out on support without the father of your children being around, I think having an extended family is twice as important. They are the ones that I get true support from, even though we have our ups and downs. I'm back in the UK now and I miss them terribly.

I decided to come back because I had met somebody and I thought we were going to get married. By the time we got home, his family had turned him against me, so here I am, with a new baby, having to live on benefits. I'd love to be working, but I couldn't afford the childcare costs with two children. There's a lot of resentment about people not working, but they don't know how difficult it is to pay for your childcare. So I'm going to try to train for something, do some studying, so that when Bradley is getting to playgroup age, I can start to work again. I can't wait.'

For Alex, motherhood has brought new perspectives into her life as a working woman: *'I think I've changed enormously since having children and more so after each baby. I've finally realised that the company won't collapse without me. You know the way you think that nobody else can possibly do that bit of your job, but maternity leave has shown me that my presence isn't essential.*

I don't get as nervous either, I'm less uptight and I think that's because I'm able to see things in a wider context. It seems to me that this has made me a better manager: I'm more human, which helps because I've got 16 people reporting to me.

I don't really separate work and home: lots of people think of other things while they are at work, so why not think about your family? I don't see them as two separate areas of my life, it's more of a continuum. I'll take work home to be with the family, or I'll ring the nanny during the day to see how the children are.

Sales and marketing is quite a young profession – there are more single, childless people than there are mothers. I'm not torn about socialising with them because I don't have a great deal in common with them – I'd rather go home than go to office functions.

When I was childless, I used to stay late. When I first returned to work I used to feel guilty about not staying late any more. Now I really feel that quality is better than quantity.

I feel that fathers may experience more problems with not staying late, for example if their partner has just had a baby, they're still expected to be at work until 10pm. It's easier for a mother to say no, particularly if she's breastfeeding, or has to pick up from a childminder.'

Eleanor tried to be everything to everybody but had to stop: *'I didn't make a decision to return to work: it just happened. We had been trying for a baby for two years and had been to the fertility clinic, but nothing was happening. I was at the stage of having weekly scans which was becoming very disheartening. My whole life became dominated by it.*

So I tried to accept that children were once in the equation, but now they're not. It helped to focus my mind on work and my career, but of course, as soon as I did this I became pregnant. It was hard to believe and I thought something would go wrong. I told myself that I'd have the baby, have a couple of weeks off and then go back to work.

I was going along at such a speed that I never stopped to consider how much time caring for this child was going to take. I thought I'd rock it under the table while I worked.

Although we'd wanted a baby for so long, now one was on the way I was determined that it wouldn't change my life. When I had her, I was on a high. Nothing happened to shake my belief that it could work – you could combine motherhood with a busy career. I was back at work full time and Rebecca was only three months old. It was wonderful – then it went off the boil: I started to notice that I was getting upset by the amount of pushing and shoving on the Tube and there were issues like moving Rebecca onto solids. It all seemed to be happening at once and I was getting more tearful. I thought maybe I'd work part time, but I was determined to finish the project I had started . . . but then the depression took over very quickly and I lost energy both physically and mentally.

I'm sure a lot of the cause of the postnatal depression was hormonal, but there were also lots of pressures on me: my husband thought he was going to lose his job; I also felt very guilty about getting pregnant – I had just gone from freelancer to salaried employee and although my boss said, don't worry, we'll look after you, I felt bad about messing them about.

The pressure on me to hold the whole thing together was phenomenal, I was taking on too many roles. I didn't wobble at all until the crisis passed. The pressure on Phil's job ended, and then I cracked, which goes to prove the theory that you keep going until you can stop.

I was in and out of hospital for six months. I felt very ashamed of letting it all go, getting it all so wrong. Rebecca stayed with me and a local nursery kept her place open for her until she could go there. Although Phil was marvellous he never let on to his boss what was happening; they may have given him compassionate leave to look after Rebecca, who knows.

We were the first of our peer group to have a baby and didn't know what to expect. Now my best friend is pregnant and I say to her, don't put yourself under pressure. I wish someone had told me that. I went back for three days a week after that.

Now I have two children and the balance has tipped. Phil is earning that much more, and our relationship has matured. My intention is to go back to work but it's a horrible choice to make. I realise now that I can't do them both, I can't work full time and parent full time.'

Pat, too was convinced that life would be the same: '*When you have your first baby, you have no idea how it will change your life. You think you can go on with the same things – and if you have a career you don't want to give it up. I found life at home quite difficult during those first few winter months; I felt cooped up with Ben and I hadn't built up a network of support. It wasn't a great wrench to go back to work, I must admit.*

Then Adela was born when Ben was four. By that time I had joined the Working Mothers' Group and my view on children had changed, through contact with other working mothers and the increasing pleasure of having Ben: he was more interesting by now, wanting to talk to you, read to you and so on. I took voluntary redundancy when Adela was born and the idea of the family became more important. I feel now that as children get older, they need you more.'

Lydia's return to work filled her with horror: '*Oliver was born six weeks early. I was shell-shocked from the early arrival and the caesarean delivery. I had problems breastfeeding and felt very depressed. I work in a bank and we had a bank mortgage, so I knew I had to go back, but the thought of returning filled me with dread.*

My attitude had changed overnight. I felt that the job wasn't worth while, it had no value, it was just a job. Before, I hadn't really thought about it, but now I was convinced that bringing up a child was far more important than any other job.

I was reluctant to go back, but the bank were very flexible with my working hours and it looked as though I could fit my part-time work into three days, if I worked through most of my lunch hours.

But then, three weeks before I was due to go back, my husband Sam was made redundant. It seemed inevitable that I'd have to go back full time but all my instincts said "no". The closer the time came the more convinced I became that I did not want to miss out on my baby's growing up.

Anyway, we managed to sort out my hours and in the end we still had enough money to live on because Sam got some redundancy money. Also, my mother offered to look after Oliver when I was working, which meant that we had no childcare costs. It helped me to know he was with her, not a stranger. I could cope with working for three days, because I knew I'd then have four days with him, so I was spending more time with him than away from him.

At first when I went back I rang mum's during the day and heard him crying. I knew that he was okay and I had just picked unlucky moments to ring.

I had to make myself not phone — I knew mum would phone if she needed me.

Being back at work isn't as bad as I expected. At first, you feel like you're two people. The old team think you're the same person, but you're not, you're more laid back. I try not to talk about Oliver, but he is the whole focus of my life. It's nice when someone does ask, but then I worry in case I talk about him too much.'

Cassie's problems began when she stopped work: *'Ian was seven months old when I went back to work. First of all I did three days a week as a computer consultant, but then I worked full time for 14 months and it nearly killed me. It wasn't just the work, but the company had relocated to premises 25 miles away, and it was the distance that was the problem. Then they told*

me that I either had to stay on full time or leave. They didn't want to set a precedent, so I had no choice, but to leave.

Although I'm glad I did, I wish I'd been able to plan it better. Ian was two and a half when I left and he'd been with a childminder until then. He was happy there, and he found it traumatic to lose his friends and the childminder's family. I think he found it very hard to adjust to the change in his life. He was bored at home with just me and I think I was too. So I got involved with the local NCT branch to get to know people, but neither of us fitted in easily.

In retrospect I should have organised something else for both of us, but I was worn out by the job, so I was pleased to stop. I would say to someone else, before making any moves: think about the timing if you do decide to give up work; think about how you will fill your day; think about yourself and what you will do, rather than just thinking about your child.'

Carolyn went back earlier than she would have chosen to: *'There is no doubt about it – I didn't want to go back to work when I did, but we were in debt, and moving to a cheaper house wouldn't have helped, because the value had dropped so much since we bought it, so there was no option.*

Ideally I would have waited until Tom was at school as well as Chlöe, but that wasn't possible. I'd also had plans to retrain as a primary school teacher, but I didn't get the opportunity to do it. I work in a college of further education, and I had heard on the grapevine that there was work around, so I felt I had to take it when it was offered.

I feel that there's someone with a whip behind me saying, faster, faster. I do seven teaching hours, but you have to triple that with preparation, and I can only do that when the children are in bed. I feel there is a high personal cost to all this preparation: I have no time to myself.

I also have this constant fear in the back of my mind – what will I do if they are ill?

But the strange thing is, much as I didn't want to go back, now I've started work again, I couldn't give it up. It's reawakened me. When we were broke and I wasn't working I had a terrible sense of impotence. However hard I tried, I couldn't make any difference. Working has helped my self-esteem, and given me a sense of contributing to the house.'

CHAPTER *three* Achieving
a balance between
work and home

MOST PEOPLE find becoming a family a life-changing experience. During your first few weeks of parenthood it is hard to envisage being able to do anything apart from look after the baby, because it is all so time consuming. Very often mothers feel as though they have changed essentially: they have different priorities, different expectations.

HOW YOUR WORKING LIFE MAY CHANGE

SO HOW does that feel when you go back to work? Is it possible to concentrate on something else while thinking about the baby all the time? How do parents strike a balance between working hard and running a stable home? What are the changes you may notice in your working life, what are the obstacles you may encounter, and what are the solutions?

One of the obvious changes is the daily routine. There is childcare to organise, more and more people to be responsible for, and to. For example, you need to liaise with people about your plans, so your spontaneity is dramatically reduced. This can take quite a lot of adjusting to. The childminder needs to know when

CHANGES

- You can't pop over the road for a drink after work with your colleagues when it's someone's birthday, unless you make copious arrangements first
- You can't stay for that extra hour to finish a project that is so nearly there
- You spend your lunch hours buying nappies and sleepsuits rather than perfume and magazines
- You can't admit to being exhausted after being up all night because your baby had colic
- You spend your breaks dashing to the rest room with your breast pump
- You are itching to get home from 4.30pm onwards because you miss your baby so much.

Change can be positive too:

- You actually enjoy office gossip now, because it gives you a chance to switch off from children
- You may feel more motivated than before, because more depends on you keeping your job
- You enjoy the company of your colleagues because you know that parenting can be quite isolating.

you are going on holiday, your child has to be picked up by a certain time, you can no longer leave the house in 15 minutes if you oversleep.

THE OBSTACLES TO ACHIEVING A BALANCE

Leaving your baby

HOW LONG does it take to believe that your baby is okay without you? For some parents, returning after the first day and finding a happy baby is enough for them to start to relax and enjoy being away from the baby. Other parents take longer than that and suffer from true separation anxiety. It can take some time to stop worrying that every action you take will have a direct effect on your child.

Frances says: *'I went back to work three weeks before I had to, because I knew it would be a busy time, and so I wouldn't have a chance to think about James as much. I think it worked. The other advantage was that I traded those three weeks with three weeks in the future for a trip to Australia when he is a year old.'*

Alex made sure that the adjustment was made slowly: she arranged to go in for mornings only for two weeks, to get both of them used to the changes. *'But when I went back I felt dreadful and it didn't stop. Sometimes it was not so bad and sometimes it was terrible. I was racked with guilt. If Rebecca was ill, I blamed myself for working full time.'*

Kerrie admits: *'The moment of separation was awful. I couldn't take Jo for the first couple of days, even though I was perfectly happy about where she was going. The first morning at work, the Personnel Officer knew I was on the edge, and didn't push me. After that I was fine, and Jo was fine too. My child-minder would ring me up at work if Jo had been upset and let me know that she'd settled down.'*

Saying goodbye

THIS DEPENDS on the age of your baby. When they are very little they may well be asleep when you go. Some parents prefer the quiet exit, which can often mean that the baby or child doesn't get upset, because there is no moment of separation. On the other hand, you run the risk that, as they get older, they will cling on to you more because they don't know when you will be going, and they won't let you out of their sight.

By saying goodbye to them you are making the point of separation clear and it may be upsetting for them, and for you too. But on the other hand, the child knows what is happening and will get a good-bye kiss and cuddle from you. It could be that once she gets used to that routine, and knows that you will go anyway, whether she cries or not, you will both benefit from an easier parting.

To ring or not to ring?

FOR SOME, it is impossible to switch off babies and onto work if the last thing you saw was your baby crying in some-one else's arms. The chances are that the baby stopped crying the minute you left, but you don't know that, and may have spent the next hour fretting about your baby's welfare.

If you ring up, you may pick the very moment that your baby is crying for some completely unrelated reason. But it won't seem like that to you, as you sit in your office, having heard her crying ringing in your ears for what seems like hours. You could ask your childminder if they can give you a call, until you start to relax about it, just as a reassur-ance.

If your baby is in a nursery it's prob-ably easiest if you ring them. After all, if there is a baby crying at the other end, the chances are that it's not yours any-way. But often another member of staff can pop through to where your baby is and put your mind at rest.

What about guilt?

WHEN I WAS talking to the mothers about this book, there were probably as many who didn't feel guilty, as did. There is a strong sense from some parents that they are enhancing not only their own lives by working, but those of their children. They would be stifled by being at home all the time, they need the outlet of work, they feel it enables them to be better mothers.

Of course, these mothers may miss their children, or feel that they are missing out on some of the fun of being a parent, but they don't feel guilty about it.

Alex did feel guilty about leaving her little girl. This was compounded by some of the reactions she got from work: *'The first time I went back, people really hurt me – they said I was just doing it for the money and what about my kids. Some people have strong opinions and feel they have to say something. It worried me because at the time I was a bit confused myself and didn't know whether I was harming her. Now Melissa has turned out fine and I have a good relationship with her. I know that I'm doing the right thing.'*

Lois went back to work when her baby was two and a half weeks old. Her parents were looking after him, and she remembers bursting into tears at her first job because she felt so guilty. Then her husband Nick pointed out that she had left him in the next best possible hands. *'I felt it was different leaving him with family, though I was upset at the time. But I had to break myself in gently when I left him with a childminder for the first time – he was fine.'*

Work, babies and tiredness

UNTIL A BABY starts sleeping through the night reliably, and this can take months, even years, for some, there are going to be times when tiredness will seem all-consuming.

Sue spent a lot of her early weeks back at work, exhausted: *'Alexandra had trouble with her ear when I started back at work, in a new job. That meant she could be awake every two hours during some nights. I was just a zombie, but nobody seemed to notice.'*

Louise's son wasn't a good sleeper: '*I used to be shattered but you carry on because you're at work. I'm now convinced it's why I never lost weight, because I used to eat myself awake. I thought that if I ate something, it would make me feel better.*'

Kerrie adds: '*Now I am constantly exhausted – I never have enough sleep. We take turns for a lie-in at the weekend. I didn't used to feel like this all the time, but it's part of the penalties you pay for working and commuting a distance too. When I get home, I don't stop, because Jo doesn't go to bed till 8.30pm, so you can't cook till then. We don't eat until about 9.15pm, so by the time you've cleared up, that's the evening gone. But instead of going to bed then I want a bit of time to relax, so I always go to bed later than I should.*'

Just a part-timer

FOR MANY people, in order to get on, you have to be seen to be working long hours. In some companies nobody leaves work at six, even if they've done everything. It is not the done thing to leave on the dot.

So where does that leave working parents who have to get away on time for their children? For those parents who go back part time the long hours culture simply isn't worth the sacrifice that has to be made in terms of family life. But that doesn't make it an easy decision to become a part-timer.

Harriet had qualified as an accountant eight years before her daughter Olivia was born: *'It had taken me years to get where I was. I didn't want to give up. I also wanted an element of independence – we live within the grounds of my husband's work, and I wanted some contacts away from that. I made it quite clear that I would be coming back, and I planned to go back full time, until I actually returned.*

I went back full time after six months, but the recession was biting our company, and there wasn't much work about. I had given up clients when I left and it was hard to build up more.

When I suggested going part time for a while, they were very keen on the idea and so I started working mornings only which went very well for a couple of months. But then a big contract came up which they wanted me to take on, and so I went back in full time, but I found I was unhappy doing it: I had got used to doing part time. As Olivia was getting older, she was getting calmer, and wasn't such hard work, so I was enjoying her more.

Then they offered me the carrot of a partnership. They said: "Come back to full-time work, we'll give you the relevant experience and in two years' time . . . ". I was very tempted. I wanted to feel that I had achieved something, reached the pinnacle. So I said I'd go back, but I wasn't prepared for my feelings. I reached the end of the first week having worked from 7am until 7pm and I knew that this was how it would always be if I was going to make it as a partner. I was very tired, very grumpy, and there were so many things to be done at home. But the worst thing was that I had lost touch with Olivia already. I decided to risk losing my job totally and said that I wasn't interested in the partnership, if this is what it takes. It was a difficult decision to take, and it was the turning point of my career, but now I had Olivia I was able to look at the other partners and their work-dominated lives and admit that I didn't want to do it. They're very wealthy, but their work is their everything. I have more than that now.

They made it quite plain that I wouldn't progress any further, but they were happy to keep me on a part-time basis for the time being at least. They made it clear that in ten years' time they might have to reconsider the situation.

But then I was headhunted by a former client. I insisted on it being part time and they agreed. They were very positive about it and made it clear that it could be a job for life. This was a tax job, so I needed to go to their Head Office overseas to learn about their tax system. So all our family are going on an expenses-paid trip for five months: me, my husband, Olivia and her nanny!'

Not everyone found working part time to have as many benefits. Laura first went back for two and a half days a week: *'I found that my work got less interesting when I was back as a part-timer. It was very gradual, I didn't notice at first, but after about six months I felt I was treated less as a working person. I was told that I would make a good team leader, but "you know it's out of the question as a part-timer". I think it did affect my career prospects although the attitude from my colleagues didn't change and my ranking on ability didn't suffer.'*

DOES WORKING part time make life more difficult for a man?

Chris works as a computer programmer and when his daughter, Hannah, was about four months old, he started working a four-day week so that he could spend time with her. *'I must say that in my current work environment there's absolutely no stigma attached to being a part-timer. Certainly, more women than men work reduced hours but in my section of about 35 personnel, I know of two other males who have decreased their work hours. I don't have to justify working shorter hours. I'm just not expected to produce the same output as a full-time employee.*

In this company working part time is not seen as an obstacle to progression and promotion if an employee is capable of meeting the demands and responsibilities that a higher post in the organisation requires. In practice, I don't think there are many part-timers in the higher echelons of management. My own ambitions are pretty meagre, and I'm not after promotion particularly — work is more a means to an end, at present. In any case, I've welcomed the opportunity to get involved with the care of my own daughter. There have been a number of folk who have respected my decision to do this. I'm fortunate, of course, to have my partner, Sally, who earns a relatively high salary and fully endorses the idea of sharing childcare.'

Sometimes, people don't feel completely in the swing of things as a part-timer. Pat experienced this: *'I felt I was just coming in, doing some work and going home again – I didn't feel that I was part of what was going on. I don't know whether the feeling came from me or the company.'*

The sense of having to justify yourself, or prove yourself, as a part-timer, is very common. Eleanor felt it strongly: *'I took my baby into work once or twice and she was asleep under the desk for ages, but another woman was doing up her house and spent lots of time organising it on the phone. I must have done twice as much as her, but she commented that I shouldn't have bothered coming in with the baby.*

I felt I needed to justify my existence – to constantly increase my workload. I was late in a few times and got comments. That's why I've given up now, I'd rather do freelance and make up the time in the evenings. I don't want people to have the right to judge me about how much work I do.'

There is also this feeling, even though you're part time, that you have to do as much, if not more in your hours, than the full-timers do in a day and can never be seen relaxing. Laura says: *'I felt that I was fitting five days into the four. I didn't sit around drinking coffee first thing, I felt that you have to justify working the shorter week.'*

Amy is a GP, and is the only partner in her practice who is a part-timer: *'I feel I'm not pulling my weight 100% even though I work 30 hours a week. But having said that, I think that my job is quite family-friendly, if stressful. In this practice, all the partners except me take on extra work, like the Well Woman clinic, but I can't do that too, and I've dropped my home visits, so someone else gets paid for that.*

It means that I do feel slightly like a second-class citizen, but my family is my priority and that's that.'

MANY PARENTS feel that although they want to be back at work, they don't necessarily want to be there all the time, to the detriment of their family life. But, as we have seen, many women feel that their careers are suffering because of it. Things are changing, though, slowly, and job shares and shortened hours and working from home are becoming more acceptable.

What happens when the children are sick?

'The real problem is if the children get ill', Carolyn

'The difficult thing is not having family close by — I don't know what I'd do if she was ill', Sue

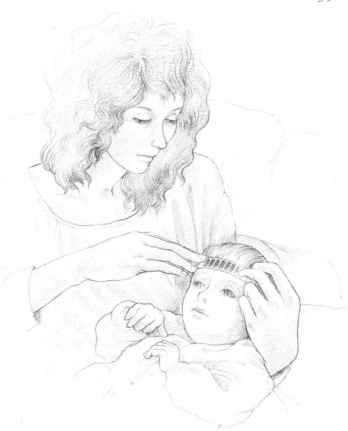

THIS IS the perennial problem of being a working parent: most of the time it runs along smoothly, but when a child is sick, there is a major strategical problem. Some companies offer a set number of days' leave each year to allow parents time off when their children are ill. Often parents have to make their own arrangements.

Sue started a new job when she returned to work from having her baby. Her little girl, Alexandra, had problems with her ear, and was due to have a grommet fitted, so she didn't know whether she would get the call from the hospital on her starting day: *'I had to tell work that it could happen on the first day, but they were okay about it. I made it clear at the interview that my family comes first — they know that anyway, and they were glad I'd been honest with them.'*

Kerrie always kept a week's leave aside, so that if Jo ever needed her, she always had a few days for that purpose. She still feels guilty sometimes, even when she is poorly herself: *'Recently, when I was ill, and so was she, we stayed in bed all day. The next day she still wasn't right, and I probably could have gone in, but I stayed at home to look after Jo. I still wasn't completely well, but I felt guilty.'*

MANY WORKING parents have a fear that if they take too much time off because their baby is sick, they might be fired. These fears may be unfounded, but rumours of it happening to others tend to haunt working parents.

If it's the minder who is ill there are a number of options: another childminder who you keep up your sleeve for such occasions, a relative, a temporary nanny or nursery place.

A support network of other local mothers can be invaluable as Jan found: *'I have two close friends who work part time as well and we help each other out when childminders are ill. We even have each other's children if they are a bit under the weather. They play together so much that if one of them is hatching something the others have probably picked it up anyway.'*

Of course if your child is really unwell it is you they need. *'When Katy was 10 months old she had primary herpes; her mouth and throat were covered in ulcers and she couldn't eat or drink. All she wanted was to suck at the breast and be carried around. There was no way I could work.'*

SOLUTIONS

Coping with separation anxiety

THERE ARE WAYS that you can make the separation easier for both you and your child, but the important message is not to feel you are being immature or neurotic. Try:

- Building up the time spent with the carer slowly.
  Start by staying with the carer for a while, then, as your child gets to know the carer, try leaving them alone for longer periods of time.
- Leaving familiar objects with her.
  If she is going somewhere else, take her favourite toy, blanket, anything that will give her that extra security.

● Establishing routines.

Babies and children all like routines because it gives them control in their lives and a sense of security. Make it a habit to explain what is happening next from the earliest days and as soon as your child can understand you, which is probably earlier than you think, they will already feel more relaxed. At the beginning of the move back to work, try to keep as many other things the same as possible, so your child doesn't have to make any more adjustments than are necessary.

● Making sure that you are completely happy with the childcare.

It may sound obvious but it really does make a difference if you feel totally happy that your baby is in the right place. And she is likely to sense your security or insecurity about the carer.

COPING STRATEGIES

Checklist

1. Be happy with your arrangements.
2. Prepare everything in advance, so the morning isn't a mad rush. Pack changing bag, change of clothes, etc.
3. Try to arrange a shortened day at first.
4. Make sure you know what you are expected to take – or leave behind.
5. Give your carer your phone number at work, and extension number.
6. Talk to your carer the day before you start, when your baby isn't around.
7. Warn your employer that you may be a little late.
8. Avoid planning meetings for first thing in the morning.
9. Take plenty of tissues, make-up replenishments.
10. When you say you are going, take a deep breath, and go.
11. Find a quiet spot to have a good cry if you need to, blow your nose and tell yourself that she'll be fine.
12. Debrief how you feel with your partner or a friend.

Negotiating

IF YOU are not totally happy with the arrangements for your return to work, there may be room for negotiation.

Laura says: *'My sort of job (in inflation management) costs the employer about £20,000 to get someone trained up. It has got to be worth getting people back. But if you are the employee, it takes confidence to ask for changes. If you're going to ask, you need to make sure that you're asking the right person. There is no point in asking someone who has no time for working mothers. My boss is a woman, she has a little girl, but she is not terribly supportive. She says things like, "I never think about Rebecca". Because she is a working mother, you would expect her to be more sympathetic to others and their feelings.'*

On the other hand, many mothers have had more success than they expected by being firm, like Helen: *'I am a social worker. I was due back to work when my baby was six months old, but I didn't feel I would be ready by then and I was getting very unhappy about leaving the baby. But since this was later than the original date I was due back, I felt I couldn't ask for any more time off. But then I talked it through and decided that I would ask. I suggested another two months' leave and we ended up agreeing on a compromise. This means that my baby will be eight and a half months when I go back, which is fine by me.'*

Alex feels that it's very important to negotiate for what you want, as she did after the birth of her second child: *'I went back two months early from my maternity leave and was given ten weeks to prove that I could do my job part time. They told me it was out of the question for a manager to be part time. We ended up agreeing on total flexitime. So as long as I do my 37.5 hours a week, I can do them whenever I want. Time spent travelling also counts as part of my working day. I go in very early, at 6.30 or 7am, one or two mornings a week, so that I can leave early to be with the children. And I can go back to work in the evenings, after they're in bed.*

It's tough, but it's worth it for the children. I don't think you're ever completely happy, but what I've learnt is that you have to be creative by thinking around the problem and you have to be prepared to make a series of compromises.'

Assertiveness skills

BEING ASSERTIVE is all about making your objectives and your feelings clear, in a pleasant but firm style. It's not about banging your fist on the table, or bursting into tears when something doesn't go your way. This just invites negative and demoralising comment.

Unfortunately, it is still hard to be accepted as an assertive, strong woman. Even today, assertive men are seen as 'powerful' and 'dynamic', but assertive women can be seen as 'bossy, nagging or being difficult'. Try not to be put off by the stereotyping.

If you are not used to being assertive, it can be very difficult, particularly if you have been away from work for a few months. It's amazing how quickly one can lose confidence in one's own abilities.

ASSERTIVENESS
Being assertive is: ● Knowing what you want   ● Being clear   ● Listening carefully   ● Being polite   ● Stating your case   ● Not being put off in your objective.   **Being assertive is not:**   ● Shouting   ● Being rude   ● Overriding other people's views.

One answer is to practise being assertive in your daily dealings.

For example, if you're in a restaurant and you are breastfeeding your baby, what would you do if someone complained?

Sometimes your assertiveness skills are not just needed when you are negotiating your terms of returning, but when you get back into the office. Frances says, *'When I went back to work, someone had taken over my desk. I was offered a place in the corner. I needed all my assertiveness skills during those first few days.'*

IF YOU have been away from the office for a few months, it is easy to feel marginalised by behaviour like this. If you have lost some of your confidence when you were away, and feel a bit rusty in the job anyway, you may feel they have a point. But within a few days, you are likely to be back in the swing of the office. Your colleagues will probably be delighted to have you back and see that you're the same person, but with an added dimension.

If you are interested in learning more about assertiveness there are many courses available – your local library may be able to provide contact information.

Sharing the responsibility for childcare

IF BOTH you and your partner are working, then can it be assumed that you share the responsibility for arranging care, dropping off and picking up?

Sometimes, as Kerrie relates: *'More often than not John is the one who's picked her up or taken time off. It comes down to whose meetings are more important. I'm more strong willed and say this is very important, and he usually caves in.*

   One job is not more important than the other – we are both in managerial jobs and both have responsibilities. You can't just leave things at the drop of a hat. I couldn't get home from London by 6.30pm when the nursery closes so it has to be him.'

Sometimes partners go further, and work shortened hours in order to share the parenting, like Chris: *'I can only speak for myself, but there is no doubt that the experience of looking after Hannah for a full day each week has been a valuable activity. I'm sure that the father–daughter relationship has been strengthened and my understanding of what Sally has to cope with in her everyday childcare has increased enormously. Dads that don't have the time to spend with their young children miss out on a lot. I wonder if the relationship with the female partner is strengthened by being more involved, too?'*

Louise and her husband are partners in their business, so they are more able to be flexible. She works two days a week: *'We try to make it an either/or scenario, which is nice after the breastfeeding period when it's predominantly the mother. But if one of the children were sick, it would probably be me that came home – I'm less squeamish!'*

However, others come to an amicable arrangement that the mother takes direct responsibility for all things childcare-related, like Laura: *'My husband's career takes priority – it's difficult for him to take my job seriously as it doesn't even cover the mortgage. We have a tacit arrangement as the house wouldn't run without his job. He sees things from a financial point of view. I think he's the loser, but the long hours culture means that it's hard for him to be taken seriously by his colleagues if he doesn't.'*

ALTHOUGH IT is becoming more common for men to take responsibility for childcare they are still more likely to receive recognition for their efforts than women. For example, Stuart, a barman, thrives on the attention he gets from his children's friends: *'They think it is marvellous that I am at home during the day and participate in the neighbourhood babysitting circle.'*

It isn't easy to find a balance of responsibility. It will depend on a number of factors, like:

● Your attitude to returning to work
● Your partner's attitude to your returning to work
● Attitudes and flexibility at both places of work
● Other sources of support.

IF YOU ARE a single parent, you are likely to be shouldering the whole responsibility yourself, unless you have family who can help you out. Being a single parent means that you may need the stimulus of the workplace as a balance between caring for your child single-handed and without adult interaction.

SO, ALTHOUGH most parents will agree that having children changes your life, after the first few years of intensive activity and adjustments, old habits do return and you can achieve some sort of balance between your working life and family life.

CHAPTER *four* Time off – life as a family

SO FAR, the emphasis has been on work in this book, but becoming a family is also about having time off together. Working and running a home leaves little time off for either partner; there are usually household chores to be done: cleaning, washing, ironing, shopping and more.

Add to that the fact that you are unlikely to have seen much of your children during the working hours, so you will want to spend time with them, and of course your relationship with your partner, which so often gets put to one side with the arrival of babies, will still need nurturing. How can it be possible to do all of this, and relax too?

SHARED PARENTING

WITH BOTH partners working, there should be a more equal division of labour for the other household chores, and a division of the sense of responsibility for doing them. The reality is that many women take responsibility for their childcare arrangements, while the partner may support her by helping out with pickups, or other tasks.

Kerrie relates: *'Last summer, John was very busy at work and involved in cricket . . . I said I wanted a day when he does everything and I get pampered. He's never, ever, done the whole day: he's done work days, but never a whole day at the weekend. I want him to see the ups and the downs.*

At the Working Mothers' Group, I was talking about our arrangements. I said I drop Jo off and John will pick her up, and that he's promised me that he will pick her up on time. Someone said to me: "What do you mean, he's promised you? That means you're taking the responsibility for it, and for making sure that he's done it." He's making the commitment to me, and I take the ultimate responsibility. Which is true and I think that most working mothers would admit that they are the ones who feel responsible. I do.'

Sometimes things can start off equally, then drift. Caitlin admitted that: *'My husband doesn't help around the house, but he does like to cook, so he usually prepares the meal in the evening. I think the shared parenting idea has reduced as time has gone by. He was full of enthusiasm at first, but less so now. But he does come home every lunchtime, so he gets to see the children then.'*

SOMETIMES BREASTFEEDING can change the dynamic of a relationship that has been working equally by sharing all other events before the baby. Some fathers might not bother to get up during the night if they feel they are superfluous. On the other hand, some fathers give bottles of expressed milk in addition to the mother's breastfeeding. Or, if their baby is still waking up at night, the father may get up and bring the baby to the mother for feeding.

Shared parenting as a skill to be learnt

MOST OF us have been brought up with certain assumptions, and may have adopted certain roles, almost without thinking about it. A lot of these role models come from our parents, who lived in different circumstances to us in many cases. So when we think about shared caring, and maybe wonder in a disgruntled way why we end up doing so much, it could be worth thinking about our own assumptions, and those of our partners, and start working from there.

Communication is all in these circumstances, particularly where assumptions may be made. Male partners and their responsibilities have changed enormously over the last thirty years, even though to some people they may not seem to have done. Not only that, but what is total inequality of responsibility to one couple is shared parenting to another – things that were totally unacceptable as a father's role some years ago are now treated as natural, such as cooking meals on a regular basis, or bathing the children, but people don't change at the same pace. You need to be sure you are not making assumptions about your own relationship, by sitting down and talking about what is important to you both.

Casting a new light

'It incenses me that women are criticised for being scatterbrained, or bad dri-vers. It's because they are doing so many different things at the same time, and doing most of them well. No wonder things get forgotten. But men can ignore one thing, like when you're lying in bed, and the baby is crying – he will turn over and not respond. The woman always cracks first,' says Eleanor.

THIS TYPE of friction can come about because partners feel that the other one isn't pulling their weight, or they are expecting too much. Until the couple become a family, there has been no need for a debate about this. Then all of a sudden, there is a new baby, the famil-iar autonomy is removed, and the couple's role model roots suddenly appear along with assumptions. Sometimes people aren't necessarily aware of their own assumptions until parenthood happens to them. Once you perceive yourself as a mother or a father, you can sudden-ly step into your parents' shoes and behave in the way that you asso ciate with parenthood, without having come to a reasoned conclusion that it's the best way. Have you ever heard children imitat-ing their parents: wagging fingers, or copying those timeless expres-sions? That's what can happen when you become a parent: you find yourself repeating all those daft things that your parents said to you – that's my girl . . . wait and see . . .

It is easy to have an equal relationship when you are both earning a salary, working full time, have no dependants. How will you feel if, because you stay at home with your baby, for a few weeks or a few years, you are automatically cast in the role of the housewife?

Allocating tasks

IF YOU want to share the parenting, think about what needs doing. Allocate tasks according to what times you are around, or what you are best at doing, or what you prefer to do. After all, nobody is like-ly to want to take responsibility for all the jobs they hate. But you could list everything that needs doing and decide what you can take on.

You could list these in order from one to three, say, of preference, with one being most favoured. Those jobs that only you like, you do,

and those jobs that only your partner likes, the partner does. And those jobs that you both hate, you alternate on a weekly basis.

Many couples find that having someone to help in the house eases the pressures. Even though money is tight Karen pays a neighbour to do the ironing: *'Just looking at the laundry basket used to make me feel cross. Now I drop it off on the way to work and pick it up later. It's worth £3 an hour not to have to start ironing at ten o'clock at night.'*

Alex accepts that she is prime childcare organiser, which suits her and her husband very well, but she expects him to take a role in other areas: *'I am the prime organiser. I pay the nanny, organise all childcare duties. But I'm responsible for the washing, and he does the shopping.'*

Sue is happy that she and her partner share responsibilities, but she says: *'There is nothing that he can't do instead of me. It puts too much of a strain on me otherwise. One of the best things I ever did was explain to him that he doesn't help with the chores, we share them.'*

UNEXPECTED EVENTS

SOMETIMES AN unavoidable event places people in roles that they hadn't wanted at all. Joan experienced this when her husband was made redundant: *'Trevor helped out more at home, and learnt that he was doing it for our joint needs, not just to help me out. But he is working again now, albeit shorter hours, which means he can work a lot more from home, and take the children to school, and so on. I see his relationship with them warming and improving all the time, it really feels more like a family.*

I did find it difficult at first to relinquish the running of the home. I had been in charge and I had to accept that we were sharing this now, which meant accepting that Trevor might not do things my way. He is very good, and things get done, but not as I would have done them.

I am, though, the prime wage earner, the prime childcarer and the main cleaner. Sometimes I wish he would just give up; he could look after the children and I could concentrate more on my job, I'd be happy with that. But I know he won't.'

CHANGING PRIORITIES

IT CAN put a lot of pressure on a relationship to have both partners carrying careers all the time, particularly when there are young children around. For some, it is easier to alternate the dominant career, so that it is possible to take a back seat whilst caring for young children, without feeling that you have to give up work for ever.

Sue says: *'We've sort of taken the decision that his job comes first, so if Alexandra was ill, it would be down to me to take care of her. It's not been a discussed decision, but we both feel happy with it. I wouldn't want to give up completely, but I'll keep ticking over until the children are at school.'*

Some couples plan such career changes to accommodate a family. Jenny worked long hours in a very demanding area of medicine, her husband's job involved lots of travel: *'Two stressful careers in one family would have been too much. Once the children were born I moved into part-time work. My career is on hold for a while.'*

NOT EVERYBODY'S job lends itself to this sort of flexibility but, as time moves on and more women want to be able to combine family and career, hopefully more employers will create a 'family-friendly' structure to their contracts of employment.

PARTNERSHIP PRESSURES

THERE IS no doubt that having a family puts pressure on a relationship, even when it enhances it in a broader sense. There is less time to go around, and the time that used to be spent relaxing with one other person is often spent chasing children to bed, reading endless bedtime stories and ironing clothes for the next morning. This doesn't leave

much time for the couple to maintain their closeness. On the other hand, if you are both working, you are likely to want to spend as much time as possible with the whole family, rather than pretend that it's just the two of you still. So where do you get the time from? How do you make time for everything? How do you avoid the symptoms of stress – tiredness, lack of libido, loss of intimacy, and conflicts over children?

One thing that can reduce such pressures is if you both feel that you have the same objectives overall.

Laura: *'It was a mutual decision for me to return to work. He definitely felt it was right for me. The only thing he would change is the method of child-care: a nanny, so there's not so much housework to do.'*

Harriet: *'My husband was very supportive about me returning to work. He prefers me to have contacts outside the house; he's always respected me for that, and he wants it to carry on. He doesn't want to lose the person that he married.'*

Amy: *'I had a lot of encouragement from my partner to go back to work. He didn't like the idea of me being concerned only with the domestic/house issues. I felt the same way, but less so now with four children. When the first two were little I felt frustrated with no one to talk to during the day, but I feel that four keep me fully occupied, and they are getting to the more interesting stage. I am more involved in reading and learning skills. With four, there are more automatic social outlets, more structure to the day.'*

Time with your partner

WHEN YOU are both working, there is, as Eleanor points out, a sort of pecking order of who deserves the lie-in at the weekend – it's easy to start counting: *'It's all down to how hard have you worked, I've worked harder than you, how hard did you work the week before . . . it's as if there are bargaining chips: "I've got to go to work in the*

TIME

Time with your partner

- Book a babysitter once a week/fort-night. You may be tired but it's probably worth having some time alone with each other
- Go to bed early – together
- Aim to spend time together, away from the TV, on a regular basis
- Talk through differences when they arise, not when they cause screaming matches
- Listen to what your partner says: you don't have the monopoly on tiredness and hard work
- Sit somewhere where there are no children's toys visible. Or better still keep one room free of train sets, dolls houses and Thomas the Tank Engines.

morning, so you've got to get up tonight . . ." and so it goes on.' Save the arguments, sort out a flexible rota.

Lindsay doesn't find it easy to spend time with her husband: *'John and I do not have much quality time together. Very often by the time the work is done, all we can do is gaze at the TV for an hour before we go to bed. That's why we try to keep our weekends for the family. Before Christmas it was hard, because I had to go to a lot of craft fairs with my books, so Sundays became very precious. However, this is the way I want to do it, and I know that whatever I want to do, John will give me support.'*

SINGLE PARENTING AND SUPPORT

IF YOU are one of a couple, there is likely to be some kind of arrangement about sharing the jobs around the house. If you are a single parent, then the burden of that is all on you. Add to that the financial implications of only one salary coming in, and life can become very stressful.

If going out to work only brings in a fraction of money over and above what is available on state benefit, by the time childcare has been paid for it may be hard for some people to understand what motivates a single mother to work. Why go out to work if you don't get any more money than staying at home with the children? A job can be a lifeline to a mother who has sole responsibility for her charges the rest of the time. It can be very important to socialise, communicate, work with adults and have a break from family life, much as you love them. Work can provide a valuable outlet for making new friends too. There are also support groups, such as Gingerbread, to make contact with people who understand the issues of single parenting.

Jane went through a period of struggling to work and bring up two children under five on her own, after her husband left her: *'There were some evenings when I'd got the children to bed that I just collapsed into bed myself, desperately miserable and exhausted. I needed someone to talk to, unwind and crack a joke with; a woman at work mentioned Gingerbread, so after a few more weeks of loneliness I rang them – it was great to speak to like-minded people.'*

Getting the most out of your time single parent style can be difficult. Consider the following:

● Asking people to make your house the venue for meetings and
   talks
● If you can't get a babysitter regularly because of cost, find out
   whether there are any neighbours who may enjoy coming to
   babysit in return for other favours such as shopping for them, or
   giving their children lifts to school
● Doubling up with other friends with children so your social life
   isn't wall-to-wall parenting.

FAMILY ACTIVITIES

THERE IS also the family as a whole whether you're a single parent or
in a couple. If the children aren't seeing a great deal of you during the
week, you may well want to spend time with them at the weekend.
But you're tired too. What can you do?

PARENTS' TIME-SAVING IDEAS

Effective time management can ease the day-to-day pressures and allow you time to be yourself again. Try some of the following:

- Splash out on a dishwasher and/or freezer
- Eat your main meal at lunchtime so that you only need prepare a snack in the evening
- Invest in a cleaner/ironing helper
- Do a weekly menu before you go shopping
- Avoid shopping at weekends – one of you do it one evening with a shopping-list
- Try to avoid taking the children shopping. They get bored before you and you end up having to leave – only to come back again a few days later
- Buy as much as possible through mail order
- If you have a nanny, get her to do as many jobs as possible, like posting letters, collecting dry-cleaning. All things that can involve taking the children for a walk
- Get your nappies delivered
- Make lists and cross things off when you've done them
- Switch the television off when you've finished watching a specific programme.

Very often, spending time with your children and getting involved with their sort of activities can be invigorating for you – it often involves exercise, which stimulates your system and gives you extra energy. It also means that the children are enjoying themselves, and we all know that happy children make for happy parents.

If you have friends with young children, try to meet up with them regularly. The children will have playmates, and you will have other grown-ups to talk to – an alternative to the extended family.

Try spending some time together as a couple while your friends mind all the children, then swap roles. Very often, double the number of children does not mean double trouble – the reverse in fact.

There are not many parents who can say they have enough time to do all the things they want to do, and it is usually sleep and 'me' time that get given the lowest priority.

Working can actually provide moments of time to yourself: travelling by train to a meeting; spending a little longer at coffee breaks;

lunch hours when you have them; all in the knowledge that your day-dreaming won't be interrupted by distant wailing.

Joy talks about her working days: *'Having worked both at home and in an office, I know the value of a lunch hour where you can sit and do a crossword and unwind. You don't get that when you're at home with children.'*

Then there is the question of guilt – should you feel that you want time on your own? If you are working, shouldn't you spend all your spare time with the family? *'I would like to take a couple of days off, to make some curtains. But then I feel guilty that if I do have a day off, I should spend it with Jo,'* says Kerrie.

THAT'S ONE of the main issues for working parents: finding the time to do everything well and meet all needs. But work can be a vital part of family life, and the fulfilment it brings can complete the picture for many parents, making it a positive and productive experience. Beth sums it up: *'I know that I'm a better person for working. I never had a picture of myself as a full-time mother, and I feel that I give more to my children by having my work role as a complement to my role within the family.'*

CHAPTER *five* Thinking about childcare

INITIAL THOUGHTS

BEFORE HAVING children, childcare is not something most people spend much time planning. Why should it be, unless you have friends in that situation, and have seen the deliberations that they are making? After you have children and if you are planning on working, the next step is to find out about the available childcare. This may be something that you start to think about when you are pregnant, if you plan to take your maternity leave and then return; or you may be looking at it when your youngest child has started school and you feel you now want to re-enter the employment market.

Have there been other people in your workplace who have taken maternity leave and said they were coming back? Did they come back, or did they decide in the end that they preferred to spend longer at home? What were your feelings about that? Were you surprised that someone would be prepared to give up a good job, just to stay at home? Or were you thinking that you might feel the same way, and how difficult the choice would be?

What about parents who return to work and have to leave at a certain time to pick up their children? Sometimes it can cause resentment amongst the rest of the workers, though most parents agree that they work harder than they did before in order to justify the stricter hours that they must keep.

When these things happen at work before you have a family yourself, they seem less relevant to you. People sometimes try and imagine how they might feel when they are pregnant, and make plans for the future; for example, the time of returning to work, or the mode of work, but often the reality of feelings doesn't come until after the baby has been born. This means that, much as you aim to be prepared for the future and arrangements about the baby, sometimes the emotions can put a temporary 'hold' sign around your plans. You may experience feelings of 'I know I'm going to feel differently once the baby is born, and I don't know how I shall feel, so I won't bother to do anything until I've had the baby and know what I want'.

However, life isn't so simple, and there are some plans that simply cannot wait until your baby is born: for example, many nurseries are booked a year or so in advance. If this is what you have decided you want, it may be too late to book by the time the baby is born. But by being prepared for any conflicting emotions you have a better chance of dealing with them when the time comes.

CHILDCARE CHOICES

THESE DEPEND ON a number of variables that will be specific to you, including your location and your particular needs.

Local conditions and availability of childcare

IN OTHER words, it all depends on where you live. When you start thinking about childcare, you need to find out what is available to you. For example, if you live in a rural area, with little public transport, you may find it more difficult to employ an au pair, who is likely to want access to English classes and an active social life with other young people.

What about childminders? If you live in a highly populated urban environment, you may find that childminders are hard to get hold of because of the demand for them. And so on. So it's worth, initially, finding out exactly what your choices are.

Each of the following will be described in more detail in later chapters.

Childminder

CHILDMINDERS ARE self-employed and care for children outside the child's home. They generally do their caring in their own homes, and have families of their own. They are registered with the Social Services and have to meet their requirements. They are inspected by the Day Care Officer of the local Social Services annually and have to meet the requirements upon which they were registered.

They charge between £1.50 and £2.50 per hour (these charges may vary regionally) and hours can be negotiated with the individual.

Nanny

A NANNY is likely to have a qualification in childcare, or be very well experienced. The stereotype image of a nanny is of an older woman in uniform pushing her charge along in a well-sprung pram.

The majority of nannies are likely to be quite young but with a qualification and experience in childcare. They may either live in, or come in daily. The cost could be somewhere between £100–£250 per week (this is net – tax and National Insurance are payable on top of this). Some expect a car and other benefits.

Au pair

AN AU PAIR is likely to be a visitor from overseas. She will live in the home, and be responsible for domestic tasks as well as childcare. But she is unlikely to have any qualifications in childcare. Her purpose for being in the country is to learn the language and culture.

In return for a 25-hour week, her minimum amount of pocket money is £35.

Nursery/workplace crèche

A NURSERY IS an organisation devoted to childcare and is likely to be run by a combination of qualified and unqualified staff. Their aim is to give babies and children a secure and stimulating environment within which to grow and develop. You can place your child in a nursery if she is between birth (or not much after) and five years old, and they have set opening and closing times. They might cost £15–£30 per day.

A workplace crèche is a nursery which is for the employees of an organisation. It will often be subsidised.

Mother's help

A MOTHER'S HELP is unlikely to have formal qualifications and you could expect them to do a bit of everything, including childcare.

They may come from overseas and would expect to be paid about £100 per week live-in, or £120 per week live-out.

Economics – what can you afford?

ONCE YOU know what you can choose from, you need to see what you can afford. Is this going to come out of one or two salaries? What will your salary be on your return? The same? Or are you doing part-time hours that will affect it? Are there any subsidised choices, for example a workplace crèche? State-run nurseries are few and far between and there may be a long waiting list.

You need to remember that if you are choosing a nanny and she is not registered as self-employed, you will be her employer and there-fore will have to pay tax and National Insurance on top of her net salary, so you need to add that on in your calculations.

If you are returning with more than one child, which is the most cost-effective method of childcare? Check whether options available offer reductions on more than one child.

Consider also the broader aspects. For example, an au pair is prob-ably the cheapest form of childcare, but she is unlikely to have expe-rience in babycare, so although it would be cheap, it wouldn't necessarily be the best for you and your family.

Proximity to office/home

THIS MAY BE something you want to consider. What is better for you – for the childcare to be more office based or home based in location?

If you are taking sole responsibility for dropping off and picking up, then maybe closer to the office is best. But if your partner is likely to be involved too, then home based may be better.

How old is your child/baby? If they already have friends, then maybe closest to home gives them the opportunity to keep up those links. On the other hand, if your baby is going somewhere for the first time, and particularly if you are still breastfeeding, would it make more sense to arrange the childcare close to the office? See Chapter Eleven for more information on breastfeeding and working.

Do you want domestic help too?

THIS COULD influence the choice of carer too. A childminder is unlikely to give you a hand with the ironing. Many nannies could be expected to do all the children's washing and ironing but not yours. An au pair could be expected to do 'light housework', and so on.

Maybe this is the time to think about how you organise your household in general. Your free time with your family will become even more precious, so maybe you could get a cleaner in once a week. Again, it could be something to include in your budget.

A carer to fit your workstyle

HOW WILL you be working?

If you are working from home, would you rather that your child was cared for out of the house all the time, to prevent the temptation a) to take over if the child is upset, undermining your carer, or b) to let your child disrupt your work schedule?

Or would you prefer to have the child close by, so that you can benefit from the proximity, stopping for lunch together, and so on?

You may need a different type of care if you work part time to full time. Some nurseries, being oversubscribed, will only offer full-time places, or only specific part-time options. They may be too limiting for you. Some childminders are not keen to pick up after school and look after children at the end of the school day, when they are tired and sometimes difficult.

Evening work brings its own issues. If you are a couple, then your partner may well be around in the evening to take over the childcare. This is certainly a cheap option financially, but you may pay a high price in terms of the relationship, because you are likely to see very little of each other.

If you are a single parent working in the evenings, this may not be an option. You would need to consider whether you could take the child with you. Hospitals, for example, sometimes have 24-hour nurseries. Otherwise you would need to get someone into the home, as minders will be looking after their own families, and of course nurseries are shut.

Access to a car

IF YOU HAVE a car, most choices within financial limits become available, and you don't have to limit yourself to a carer on a bus or train route. If you don't have a car it could be worth thinking about the benefits of a carer coming into the house, weighing convenience against additional cost.

If you do not have access to transport, maybe a bit of lateral thinking and organisation can give you what you need. What about neighbours? Could anyone be persuaded that they'd love to be a childminder for your child? Are there any retired people living nearby who may like to earn a bit of extra money? What about older teenagers, particularly those with some experience with little ones? They may have younger brothers and sisters that they're used to caring for, or their own parents may be close by to give back-up if needed.

Is there a primary school close by? Sometimes they will know people living locally who are able to look after children. Of course, if anyone is looking after your children outside your home, you should make sure that they are registered childminders, particularly if you don't know them. It is illegal for a non-relative to care for a child up to the age of 8 for payment, for more than two hours a day. What about local churches? Is there anyone the local vicar or priest knows? Is there a mother and toddler group attached to the church? Maybe you could start going for a while, and talk to one of the organisers. She may be able to help. But by making a few enquiries by word of mouth, you may pick up some useful information, and, if someone isn't registered as a childminder, then perhaps they would be prepared to do so.

Sometimes help comes from the unlikeliest of sources so let people know what your needs are, and see if there is any response. Talking to your neighbours about this is another way of getting to know them, of course. If they are unable to help you out with this, the contacts made can only be good: as a source of new friends and of support, in both directions.

You can think about your key needs, such as the above. Talk to people who have been in the same situation. What were their remedies?

DIFFICULT TIMES

THIS CAN BE a very difficult time for parents: just when you think you are coping with parenthood and all the attendant stresses you are faced with yet more decisions. You may feel lacking in confidence at first when it comes to knowing what is best for your child, you may be feeling ambivalent about returning to work and not ready to choose who will be right to look after your child. It is worth remaining open-minded when trying to make your decision – if the nursery you particularly wanted is oversubscribed don't be put off – you will find the right place.

Remember everything can be changed, nothing has to be permanent. Although it's not ideal to make changes, it is far better to do that, and make both you and the child happier, than put up with a mistake in order to avoid disruption.

Most importantly, give yourself time. Finding the right person may

CHECKLIST

Checklist of people to contact

1. Local Social Services for lists of child-minders and nurseries
2. Parents at Work (address at end of book) for helpline information on childcare and maternity rights
3. Local nanny agencies for nannies, au pairs, mother's helps
4. Local Further Education colleges to place ads for nannies at colleges with childcare courses
5. Personnel dept of company for information on company policies on maternity leave and for information on workplace crèche option
6. Local NCT group and Working Mothers group for support and networking
7. Your health visitor who may be able to suggest childminders, local crèche, etc.

happen overnight, but it may take longer, and it is good to have the flexibility to cope with that, rather than feeling that you are being backed against a wall.

You need time to be able to try the different options on offer, to see what they are like in reality. Do a few test runs: sometimes the arrangement doesn't work straight away, but you can see that things may improve with time. Sometimes you know that you have made a mistake, so you need to change your plans. Ideally, you should give yourself enough time to do this before you go back to work. It takes a tremendous amount of pressure off you. Once you have found the right place, you can relax, letting your child go there for a few hours a week maybe, slowly building up to the big day.

Start your search by ringing round agencies, or Social Services departments, place ads in the local paper, or *The Lady* if you are looking for a nanny, talk on the phone to eliminate non-starters, and begin to interview candidates.

QUESTIONS TO ASK YOURSELF

IT'S PROBABLY a good idea to start listing the things that you want from your childcare, to help you to identify the best option for you. Here are a few suggestions of the sort of things that you could look at:

- Do you want someone with a similar lifestyle to yours, or someone who might offer a contrast: other young children around or pets for example: *'I wanted my childminder to have a different lifestyle, so my children would look forward to the contrast. The minder had lots of animals, and used to take Jamie to the livestock market.'*
- Do you want someone with the same sort of beliefs as yours, so that you can relate to them? What about any religious preference?

- Do you want someone to clean up while you are out at work?
- Will you be sending one child, or more? Do they have the same needs?
- Do you want someone young and energetic, or would you prefer someone more mature?
- Do you want a male or a female carer? One of the mothers interviewed sent her child to a workplace nursery where her main carer was a male. It worked very well. There are also (few and far between) some husband and wife childminders
- Food: do you want to supply it, or are you happy to leave it as the responsibility of another?
- Are you organised in the morning?
- Do you want your child to have the constant companionship of other children or would you prefer a one-to-one situation?
- Do you want there to be an active, child-centred atmosphere or a homely one, where your child fits in with the daily schedule of the carer: going shopping with her, picking up other children from school?
- How much flexibility do you need from your carer?
- Is their attitude to breastfeeding/feeding a baby with expressed breast milk important to you? *'I preferred to have a nanny at home, rather than breastfeeding and expressing and taking it to the nursery. I feel there's a fine line between being a wonderful, wholesome mother and feeling a complete fool in front of someone else who I might have to hand it over to at a nursery. If you're breastfeeding, you're not objective. The thought that somebody might find it repulsive is strange to you.'*
- Do you want someone who will also babysit for you in the evenings?
- Is it important that your partner gets on with the carer too?
- Are you worried that there may be a personality clash in a one-to-one relationship?

Try making contact with as many relevant organisations and people as possible, so you get the broadest view of things. Talk to other parents and find out what sort of questions they asked. By compiling a list and drawing up a chart, you can begin to see a pattern emerging of your preferred type of childcare.

Important factors	Workplace	Nursery	Ch'minder	Nanny
Close to me	★			
Making local friends		★	★	
Family atmosphere			★	★
Able to leave EBM (Expressed breast milk)			★	★
Able to babysit				★

SELECTING AND INTERVIEWING

YOU WILL find more detailed information about interviewing technique, questions to ask the interviewee, and so on, in Chapter Eight. But here the broad issues of selection and interviewing are looked at.

Many people have never chosen someone to work for them before. Their job may not involve taking on new members of staff, they have never needed a cleaner, a gardener or anyone else to work around the house.

Selection

ONCE YOU have established the types of care available to you, how do you decide whether you want to go any further with them? You need to have a short list of criteria that must be met before you can proceed further with the selection. On what criteria do you base the selection? This will be personal to you, but you may include: proximity to home, or numbers of children already being minded, or whether the minder smokes. If you have thought about what are essential requirements for your minder, then it will be easier to eliminate the applicants who don't fall into that category. And you needn't feel guilty about rejecting people because you set these criteria before you spoke to anyone.

What may happen is that you will advertise and will get responses by telephone. Keep some postcards by the telephone to fill in details when people ring. Make sure you have a list of key questions or criteria ready to ask everyone.

There are agencies who deal with nannies, mother's helps, au pairs and so on. They should be able to manage the selection procedure for you. If you do employ an agency, then make sure that they do the work. For example, ensure that they have current contact with the candidate. Maybe she filled the bill two years ago, but the agency should check that her details are still the same.

Be specific about your criteria. If they start sending you CVs of candidates who don't fit your criteria, then there should be a very good reason, or they should stop immediately. If they don't do so, then use a different agency. Like everything else, there are good and bad agencies, but there are enough of them to allow you to be choosy.

Interviews

WHEN YOU are interviewing, don't forget to:

1. Plan where you will hold the interview
2. Make a list of topics you want to cover and key questions
3. Ask open questions
4. Listen to the candidate's replies – what is she not saying?

Amy says: *'The best qualified person is not necessarily the best person for the job – some people have a natural affinity. The best nanny I had didn't have any qualifications, and started looking after three of my children when she was 17 years old.'*

What do you want to find out? Sounds obvious maybe, but are there things you want to know but feel would be an invasion of privacy? Lots of people feel uncomfortable with asking personal questions. Alex did too, but she found it was a means to an end and got used to it: *'I felt awkward initially about asking questions but lost my inhibitions when I saw that the questions gave incredibly revealing answers, which I wouldn't have got otherwise. I asked one childminder if she was planning to have any more children, to which I got the answer that in fact she was pregnant at the moment. She wouldn't have told me that but it made a big difference to whether I wanted to use her or not.'*

ANOTHER IMPORTANT exercise is to notice what the candidate asks you – that can be a good pointer to what her priorities are. Hopefully, she will ask you about your children, their likes and dislikes, rather than how much you will pay her!

Where are you conducting the interview? If you are choosing a childminder, remember that it's not just the minder, but her house, how clean it is, how much space the children can use, whether it has a garden. Ria chose someone whose house looked comfortably untidy, with lots of toys out. What are the other children or her own children like? If that's important to you, ask if you can visit her when they are all around, but don't be surprised if she's not too keen for you to visit after school, when chaos is likely to reign and all the children are tired.

CONTRACTS

IT'S PROBABLY a good idea to agree to a contract when entering into an agreement with any kind of carer for your child. In this you can put all the stipulations that you and the carer have, and it's then a useful document for referral if there is any disagreement about terms. It can be as simple or as complex as you like, but it should include salary, notice agreement, hours, and holidays. There is a sample contract for a nanny on pages 120–121 which is very detailed. It gives an indication of what you might want to include.

Ideally, you and the carer should draw up the contract together, so that you are both happy with the terms.

Sharing the risks and responsibilities

BY PLACING your child with a carer you are sharing responsibility and exposing her to new risks. This realisation can evoke feelings of guilt in a parent, but with time and a carer you trust this new relationship can be beneficial to all parties.

Sylvette talks about how she felt: *'Before I had Emma, I didn't think about the guilt, the questioning and feeling torn. Emma settled into her child-care very well, but I wondered what was going on in her mind, although on the surface everything was okay. It got easier, but it took longer than a couple of weeks. I never felt totally at ease. Like lots of other things about children – it's never clear cut, there's always uncertainty. I found being a parent quite difficult to adjust to – particularly the responsibility.'*

MANY PARENTS feel totally protective towards their children and this can make choosing a carer hard. You may ask yourself – why am I leaving my child, how can I leave my child and so on. It may be that there are times when you feel that you cannot bear to leave her in the care of another. If that feeling prevails, perhaps you could consider alternatives. Most parents will feel like this at some point, so it is worth telling yourself that you are not deserting your children by organising reliable and appropriate childcare for them.

How can you be sure that your carer is totally reliable? What if the unspeakable happened and your child was injured in some way? It would be untrue to say that this never happens when you read in the newspapers that a childminder has injured a child in her care. Clearly, in these cases the wrong people are doing the wrong job. Or it could have been an innocent accident.

Part of taking responsibility for your child is by doing the best possible thing for that child. We can take all reasonable precautions but if you have a gut instinct that someone is not right for you – don't leave the child there, even if it's the last option.

Remember also that all childminders and nurseries should be registered – if they are not, don't place your child there. Nannies don't have to be registered, but you could spend time at home after the nanny starts, so you can build up a trusting relationship. Any good nanny will understand why you need to do this, particularly if this is your first child. Once you have returned to work enlist support of non-working friends. Get them to drop by unexpectedly to see what's happening – that can reassure you.

Crime programmes on TV tend to end with the presenter saying, 'Don't have nightmares – these crimes are very rare'. All a bit patronising, but true. However, you have to be happy yourself with your carer, or you will never be able to leave your child behind, either physically or emotionally.

PRECAUTIONS

Take the following precautions:

- Ask for and take up at least two references
- Check your carer is registered
- Ask around locally – a bad childminder becomes 'known' by other parents
- Do a trial run of a few hours a week before making your final decision
- Draw up a contract
- Trust your instinct
- Include a trial period and have a meeting to discuss how things are progressing.

CHAPTER *six*

Childminders

CHILDMINDERS

UNDER THE Children Act 1989, childminders are defined as 'Persons who offer a childminding service on domestic premises and for reward, to one or more children under the age of eight and to whom they are not related, for at least two hours in any one day.' Excluded from the Act are people who care for children in the child's own home (nannies, au pairs) and relatives.

A childminder is obliged to register with the local authority. There will be an officer who is responsible for registering and inspecting a childminder's home – both of which must be repeated annually. The inspection of the childminder's home would ensure that there are no safety hazards, there is enough space for children to play in and that the home is properly equipped for use by a childminder. Most local authorities will run a pre-registration course. This may include topics such as first aid, home safety, environmental health, the business side of being a childminder, child development and play, child protection issues, equal opportunities and partnership with parents.

Childminders are self-employed and they should also be insured with public liability cover, in the event of any accident happening to the child whilst in the minder's care.

CHILDMINDERS ARE usually mothers themselves, and generally, this is the way they have gained their experience. For some parents, it is this knowledge of bringing up a family that makes a childminder an appealing choice. As Alex says, *'A television programme I saw made me feel very dubious about nursery care and my baby was only going to be three months old when I went back to work. I felt that the right place for her was somewhere with a family atmosphere, so that even though I wouldn't be there, she would be in the same sort of surroundings as if I had been at home with her.'*

THE CHILDREN ACT 1989

The Children Act also sets down the maximum number of children a childminder can care for in her home. It is:

3 children under five of whom not more than 1 should be under one year (except multiple births or twins)

or

6 children between five and seven (with no under fives)

or

6 children under eight, of whom only 3 may be under five and 1 under one year.

SO FOR Alex, and many others, one of the attractions of a childminder is that their child is being cared for in a home. There are other advantages, too.

THE ADVANTAGES

Extended family

CASSIE FOUND that Andrew had made strong bonds with the minder's children, and the other children who went there too. *'My son was seven months old when he started going to the childminder, and stopped when he was two and a half. Her children became like brothers and sisters to him, and he was very much in the role of baby brother to them. He missed them very badly when he stopped going there.'* Although the advantage of the second family is clear, Cassie regrets not thinking about the timing more when she herself decided to give up work. She now wishes she had waited until Andrew was old enough to go to a playgroup, so he could make new friends quickly.

Another mother figure

NOT ONLY do children get other playmates, but they also gain a second mother figure to care for them whilst their own parents are at work. Kerrie's daughter, Jo, goes to a childminder and Kerrie describes their relationship: *'Basically she loves Jo, they love one another, she treats her as the third child she never had.'*

Kerrie finds the relationship supportive beyond their mutual commitment to Jo. *'She's my alter ego during the day. I get mail order parcels delivered to her house. We've reached the point now where if I need to change times or days at short notice she will always try and take Jo if she can – she's pretty flexible. She's got my front door key as I've locked myself out twice already. I'd never have done that before – addled brain, you see!'*

Unconventional hours

HAVING A JOB that doesn't follow conventional hours sometimes puts people off trying to get 'official' childcare. Lucy is a training consultant and may be working for two very long days, but then be home for a week. *'My parents would travel down from their home the day before the course started and stay till it finished but it was a long way to come every time. I didn't originally consider a childminder because I had been told that they only work certain hours, which seemed perfectly reasonable, because they have their own families to attend to. But then I found out that some childminders are very flexible, depending on their own circumstances. So from then on that's what I did.'*

Flexibility

ONE OF the considerations of many women is how flexible their arrangements can be. Naturally, there has to be a regular commitment to the arrangement, but some people find that a commitment that has to be made a term in advance, or that requires the same hours every day, is not the way they are able to work.

Using a childminder can solve some of these problems. They may take your child full time or part time, and, as Sylvette found, will often be flexible about irregular hours. *'I started looking for childcare when Emma was two or three months old. I had already been thinking about the options and had read quite a lot about it. I felt from what I read*

that a childminder would be best for me, because I wasn't sure of the hours I would be doing as I was starting a college course. What I knew was that I needed flexibility. I understood from the nurseries I visited that I would have to fix a certain number of days per week, and would have to pay for that throughout the year. Another thing that put me off nurseries was that I felt there could be a high turnover of staff.

I also eliminated nannies – on the grounds of cost and because most nannies haven't had children, whereas childminders usually have.

Sometimes, you have to trust your own feelings and that "gut instinct". I didn't have any luck finding a childminder in my town, and I found the whole selection process very difficult, particularly having to ask personal questions. So I contacted the Working Mothers' Group from the local NCT branch and they suggested another area that had some good childminders. I had a positive result from that, and the first minder I saw I was happy with. Why was I happy with this one? I guess it's an instinct – you know when you feel comfortable.'

Economics

RATES OF pay will vary enormously according to area and demand but it is generally accepted that childminders are the least expensive form of childcare, unless you are using a member of your family or a friend who doesn't charge. Part-time places on an hourly rate are often more expensive than full time.

Experience that counts . . .

CHILDMINDERS HAVE a strong advantage over other carers because they generally have families of their own. Some parents find this experience of mothering very reassuring, particularly with their first child, when they may feel inexperienced themselves at times.

Laura valued the additional expertise of her childminder: *'I had no problems leaving my little girl there . . . I had an excellent childminder, who showed me the way on the things I thought I was no good at.'*

IF YOU ARE a first-time parent you would probably feel happier leaving your child in the hands of a carer who has had children themselves. If you see the childminder's children are happy, well balanced and well cared for, you will feel happier about leaving your own child in her charge.

Accountability

IF A CHILDMINDER is registered with the local authority, you know that she will be following prescribed regulations and should have public liability insurance.

The Children Act obliges the local authority to satisfy itself of the 'fitness' of the childminder and anyone over 16 living on the premises.

THE DISADVANTAGES

- Some children feel more secure in the home environment, and don't want to leave that security every day
- Going to a childminder may restrict a child's social life, particularly as they get older. You could ask the childminder to take your child to the local playgroup or toddler club to avoid this.

Older children may find going to a childminder restrictive, as Emma and Beth, aged 14 and 12, point out: *'When we've been to school all day, we prefer to come back to our own house, have something to eat, just like an adult might do. If you go to a childminder, it can be boring if no other children are there, and you can't have your friends to your own house until later on.*

Children's feelings matter too. They've had a hard day too and want to come home and relax.'

- Children are likely to pick up more colds, bugs and so on if they are outside the house mixing with other children
- A less than perfect childminder may favour her own children to the detriment of your child
- You have less control over the activities in which they participate, for example, the TV may be on for longer than you would like, or perhaps there is a stash of toy guns which you had sworn your child would never play with

- If the childminder is sick, you could be left to your own devices. Some minders have their own support network and will help each other out in times of sickness, but this isn't always the case
- If you take your child to a childminder, you are the one doing the ferrying around, so your journey to and from work will be lengthened
- Sometimes mistakes are made. Your child doesn't settle for some reason or doesn't get on with that minder. That means you have to go for a complete change
- There may be a personality clash between your children and the minder's children.

A PERSONALITY clash with another child can be very difficult for the child involved, particularly if the clash is with the child of the minder, who may claim the higher ground as it is their own house. But what can be done about this?

Joan was surprised when her school–age daughter Lauren, fell out with the minder's child: '*I was looking for someone who was compatible with James as he is the youngest and hadn't been to a minder before. Diana minds Lauren as well, and there are problems there because her daughter is in Lauren's class and they don't get on. I took it for granted that there wouldn't be any issues with Lauren, because she was the older one.*' Joan listened to her daughter, and tried to explain that for her, the period of intense childcare would only be lasting for three months whilst she was on a course for her job. She treated her as a rational individual and Lauren understood and accepted the short–term nature of the problem.

EVERYONE HAS a different experience when looking for the right childminder.

Kerrie struck lucky. '*I was dreading the prospect of looking for a childminder and interviewing people – I didn't know how I was going to interview people about looking after my child, making such an important decision on the basis of a couple of hours. I didn't know how I was going to cope with it.*

But when Dee, the woman who did my ironing, offered to do it, I felt it was the perfect solution, and we knew her family too. I couldn't believe my luck. She registered as a childminder, which I felt was safer for both of us. She gave up her part-time job which she hated, and was delighted to stay at home and do what she had always wanted to do.

Dee's boys were five and three, she minded one other girl occasionally and only Jo full time. Dee takes Jo to the gym club and for swimming lessons – it's like having a nanny. Jo has this secret circle of friends who I have never met, but feel I know well. It's such a relief to me – I have absolute trust in Dee. The only time I feel guilty about what I am doing is when Jo is ill. If she's off-colour, Dee is happy to take her and will even take her to the doctor for me, but I feel bad because she would rather be with me, at least, I think so!

Occasionally she will call me Dee and Dee mummy, but they all do that, don't they? But she calls here home, and Dee's house is Dee's. I'd be more concerned if someone was in the house and she had two mother figures in the same house.

There are limitations, of course. For example, Jo can't go to the nursery I prefer because it's out of town and Dee has no transport, so she's going to one adjacent to her boys' school. You can't have everything, of course.

I pay Dee for the holidays, even though I don't have to, but I feel I'm getting a Rolls-Royce service. The relationship really works.'

Sally's experience was not so smooth . . . : 'I went back to work when Hannah was 22 weeks old. My statutory leave was 18 weeks, but I wasn't quite ready then and my employers said they were flexible, so I stayed at home for another four weeks.

I had arranged for someone to look after Hannah, but Hannah wouldn't take a bottle or go easily to other people. What I also discovered later was that although this lady was a childminder, she had very little experience of looking after babies, just older children. Hannah apparently cried all day, and at the end of the first day, the childminder said that she couldn't cope, so I had to find someone else.

Luckily, by the end of the second week I found someone else. I talked to my NCT Postnatal Supporter to see if she knew of anyone, and she knew of the right person, who was a nursery nurse and was also prepared to come to my house for the two full days that I need her. I also work on a third day but my husband, who works a four-day week, looks after Hannah that day.'

Barbara had a bumpy start to her childcare arrangements too. 'Mark is with his second childminder now. I went back to work when he was four months old, having got a minder organised in advance. He started going there before I was back at work and about two weeks before I was due back I started noticing a strong smell every time I went to the house to collect him. One day I went to the kitchen and saw a hamster's cage on the units next to the baby's bottles. That was it, so I paid her up and cancelled the arrangement.

Then I was distraught. Two weeks to go and no childminder, but I looked in a local paper, which covered the area close to my office, and found an advert for someone who had only just registered as a childminder. When I went to see her we got on very well and because she was new, she had no hard and fast rules, she just said we could sit down and discuss working together for Mark.

Mark is now one of the family. Her youngest child is ten, so Mark is the baby. He had one-to-one care for the first 18 months, then Karen took on another toddler, so now he has someone to play with.

One thing that made me think, though, was when I was there one day and *he hurt himself, badly enough to need a cuddle. He went straight to Karen. It didn't really worry me, as he was so settled there, but Karen was embarrassed.'*

WHICHEVER KIND of childcare you go for, there is a strong possibility that your child will form an attachment to one person. It's more likely to happen with a nanny or a childminder than in a nursery, but it is not unusual to hear about children confusing names: calling the minder mummy and mummy by the minder's name. Many mothers don't like it when someone else is obviously so close to their child. From a positive point of view it means that your child feels secure when she's with that person: the sort of security that she associates with you. If you know your child feels secure, you can feel more relaxed about leaving her while you work.

Sue found it was quite difficult to find a minder who would care for a baby – her daughter Alexandra was four and a half months at the time: *'They have to really want babies, because they're quite hard work. Another thing that I felt aware of is that it's not just the minders you are interviewing and questioning. It's their houses, big or small, gardens, space, use of rooms and, most of all, their standards.'*

When Ria looked for a childminder, she didn't want the ones that were too clean and tidy. She wanted her children to have free access to toys and playthings. She also chose a minder who had four children of her own, so was clearly going for the experience factor, together with a family environment: *'For Becky, this was another family. I didn't have any guilty feelings because I knew that Becky was happy there – to the extent that this was where she chose to go when I went into labour with our second child.'*

FROM THE CHILDMINDER'S POINT OF VIEW

LOTS OF women who become childminders do so because they want, or need, to work, but they are not happy about leaving their children. A morning spent discussing the role of a childminder with a group of childminders revealed a great deal about what motivates them, how they perceive themselves, what it's like to be a childminder and how they deal with controversial issues, like discipline.

Reasons for becoming a childminder vary: *'Because I like being with*

children'; 'because I don't want to leave my children to go to work'; 'because my partner/husband doesn't want me to work outside the home'; 'I needed the money'.'

Generally childminders don't take babies younger than six months old, but there is a growing trend, particularly amongst mothers who are going back to work for financial reasons, to feel that they can leave them earlier than that. It is important for a childminder to feel that they can make a strong bond with the child, and that they will be making a long-term commitment to them.

Wendy is now a grandmother, but still enjoys being a childminder. She minded brothers who are now 11 and 13. Now she is looking after their younger brother from a new relationship. *'I feel that we are ideal for each other. This mother is not the maternal type, and I am. This isn't a criticism, it's just the way things are, and we both enjoy doing what we do.'*

Advantages

MANY OF THE childminders felt there were plenty of positive points about their job, for themselves, the children and the parents.

'Mothers can return to work, knowing their children have lots of stimulation from other children.'

'A childminder doesn't get frustrated by having children around. We enjoy them and want to do lots of things with them. We will take them out to the park because when you've got lots of kids, you want to keep them happy.'

'We, as minders, benefit too, because our children have instant companions, who they miss when they're not around.'

Disadvantages

HOWEVER, THERE can sometimes be problems and disadvantages, mainly when it comes to parents and minders dealing differently with discipline.

'I have felt with some parents that there are differences over treatment of behaviour. For example, I looked after a little girl who was fine with me all day. Then, when her mother collected her she would be dreadful, and I would tell the mother this, but her mother would give her presents. I feel that was rewarding the bad behaviour, but I can say nothing about it, and it makes my job more difficult. I also feel that it undermines my authority with the child.'

'One parent told me that she never says "no" to her child, she just distracts him. But I have to say "no" to my children, and I found it very difficult to do what she wanted, which was to treat her child differently to my own children. If they were all doing something naughty, how could I not say "no" to one of them? But I talked to her about it, and in the end she accepted that I couldn't treat her child differently to mine.'

'If a parent has a problem with anything, I think it is worth bringing it up at the outset.'

ONE OF THE MOST controversial childcare issues is whether to smack or not. The general view in this group seemed to be totally anti-smacking, with comments such as: *'I'm not going down that road, even though some mothers tell me to'*; *'As a mother, I wouldn't smack my own children in front of children being minded.'*

Another area of childcare where parents and minders can some-times disagree is food. As a parent it is best to be flexible about what your child eats, unless there are obvious dietary needs or avoidances.

'I would go along with the mother's feeding requests, but sometimes it can be hard for everyone. For example, one mother brings her child's lunch every day. This causes problems because she sees what my children are eating, and she wants to eat that too, so I end up having to feed them separately.'

'A first-time mother may be horrified at the thought of her child going to McDonalds, but what if I want to take my 6-year-old there to tea one night? I did that once, and the mother gave me a pasta and bean salad for her child to eat. I gave it to her, but I'm not sure if it was very fair on her. I don't think there's an easy answer.'

There was a general consensus amongst the group that the greatest worry and responsibility is the child's safety: *'I worry in case a child ever hurt herself while I was looking after her. It would be terrible to have to tell the mother or father. We all know these things do happen, but I'd feel awful in case the parents thought I was being negligent in some way.'*

Although more and more children are starting with a childminder younger and younger there can still be problems settling – the 'clingy' stage tends to occur at around nine months. *'Generally if they start quite early, they settle in very well. They can take longer to settle back in after holidays – either school holidays or going away with their parents.'*

Suggestions for improving the child's chances of settling included: *'Get them to come in for a couple of hour-long visits'*; *'Build up slowly, with short visits together at first, then leave for 20 minutes at first and build up'*; *'Get the fathers to come too – it helps if everyone knows who's caring for the children'*.

I VISITED THIS group of childminders, they were at their weekly get-together, held in a Social Services Family Centre, which has abundant toys, and kitchen and changing facilities. It is ideal for them, because they have a chance to meet and talk, whilst their children can play together in peace (well, maybe not exactly peace . . .). These carers enjoy children and, if one minder is out of the room, then the others will meet the needs of any of the children.

They felt strongly that finding the right minder was important for everybody, and that it is worth spending time to find the right one. Your child will be fitting into their way of life, so it is important that your lifestyles, even if they are different in many respects, are still compatible.

A few points for parents to remember

SOMETIMES THE idea of the extended family can get in the way of a professional relationship. There are advantages to any child being in a home where she is treated as one of the family. But this is, after all, a job for the childminder and you are likely to keep their respect and flexibility if you do the following:

1. Have an arrangement about payment and stick to it.

2. Pick up the children on time. Obviously, trains are cancelled, and so on. But if you are late, pay extra, don't assume it's just okay.

3. Give plenty of warning about changes of plans. This is not only a commitment between you and the minder, but to the child too. If you do need to change minders, and it happens, and children survive, give them consideration and try to make the transition as smooth as possible for them.

4. Think before you speak. Deirdre is a lay organiser of local child-minders. She has to bite her tongue sometimes when asked questions like: *'Do you have any well-educated childminders?'* But otherwise she feels that mostly people are all working in the same direction. She feels that there is no invasion of privacy when asked questions. But of course it depends on how they're asked.

5. If there was any disagreement between you and the childminder, much as it may be tempting to talk about it straight away, it may be better to wait for a chance to phone in the evening, when listening ears don't get a chance to waggle too much. Unlikely though it may be, a child may play one off against the other, if she heard criticism.

6. Sometimes first-time mothers can feel undermined by a confident, experienced childminder. Whilst there are definite advantages in experience, the new mum may need time to feel her way and does not want someone telling her how it is done. It is worth spending time looking to find someone who respects your preferences and opinions, and with whom you will be happy leaving your children.

Finally the last word goes to the client on the receiving end of the childcare. Mat went to childminders once he started school. He had been at a nursery since he was a few months old until school age. Both of his parents were working in London when he started school. He is now fifteen: *'It didn't really bother me to go to childminders, because I knew that my parents had to work. There was no alternative. I had the security of knowing that I would be collected every night, plus the fact that there were other children there to play with. Although it means you can't have friends round for tea, you do have children there all the time to play with which makes up for it.'*

FINDING A CHILDMINDER

- Contact your local Social Services department. They will send you a list of local childminders, from which you can make your choice. Sometimes there will be one contact name who will suggest people close to you with vacancies, otherwise you need to contact people directly
- Ask other mothers whom you meet at coffee mornings, NCT groups and other activities
- Ring several recommended childminders and have a chat with them – this gives you an initial impression
- Decide your list of priorities and questions to ask
- Meet several, but keep an open mind until all interviews are over
- Go back and discuss details with your chosen childminder. You will need to agree on hours, rate of pay, type of payment, provision of food, notice of changes, time of drop-off and pickup, who is to provide nappies, creams, nappy sacks and anything else that you want to agree in advance. You should draw up a contract between you, so that there is something in writing if there ever is a difference of opinion
- Agree verbal or written contract
- Insist on seeing the original registration certificate and insurance certificate and make sure they are current before arranging to leave your child with the childminder.

CHAPTER *seven* Nurseries
and crèches

THE NURSERY AND THE WORKPLACE CRECHE

NURSERIES AND workplace crèches are essentially the same type of care, but there are differences in their administration: who they are there for, and who pays for them.

In a nursery, you would expect to pay the total cost, and it would be open to the public at large, whereas a workplace crèche would be specifically for the children of employees of one or more companies. Often a workplace crèche is on site, and will be subsidised by the employers, but not necessarily. Given the similarity, much of the information about both types of childcare is interchangeable.

ADVANTAGES OF THE NURSERY OR CRECHE

Stability

AN ESTABLISHED nursery is unlikely to close. There is plenty of demand for good nursery places. The benefit of this is that, although there may be staff turnover, the nursery will not change: your child will be going to the same place every day, and for some this is very reassuring.

Stimulation

NURSERIES are child-centred. That doesn't mean that nannies or childminders don't stimulate their charges, but rather that the nursery emphasis is on developing children's and babies' skills, helping them to develop, encouraging social skills. Many of the parents who opt for nurseries are persuaded by these arguments.

No boring ironing

WHILST OTHER childcarers still have to do the shopping and the household chores, the child at nursery finds that the day is geared to them, rather than when the ironing has to be done.

Surrounded by children

ONE WOMAN whom I talked to runs three nurseries and she told me: *'The children don't come here for the adults, they come here for the children. That's how children learn: by watching and playing with other children.'* A nursery certainly provides playmates, together with a number of trained staff.

Open house

IT IS WORTH talking to managers of nurseries to find out what their approach is, but most are happy for parents to drop in at any time of day to see what's going on with the children. This can be very reassuring for the parents so they can see the activities at different times of the day, and also get a chance to observe their child playing and socialising.

Opening hours improving

ALTHOUGH THEY are not completely flexible, nurseries do now have improved opening times. Each one is different, and it may not be enough for everyone, but they are usually open from 8am to 6 or 6.30pm, and some open even earlier.

Accountability

NURSERIES ARE liable to inspection from the local Social Services department, and have to be registered with them. This means that they have minimum standards to uphold, as directed by the 1989 Children Act. The Act covers issues such as safety, space for children and a separate room for babies, minimum numbers of children/babies per carer.

The recommendations for day care are:

Under twos: three children per carer;
Two to three years: four children per carer;
Three to five years: eight children per carer.

However, there are exceptions: if you choose to send your child to a nursery class which is part of a private school it does not have to comply with the standards set down in the Children Act and may not be registered.

Quality control

WHEN YOU send your baby or child to a nursery, you are likely to get a quality control stamp on their day, in the sense that they will be engaged in structured activities rather than just aimlessly playing with whatever is available. Not all nurseries will offer the same quality of care, and, like childminders, there will be some that appeal to one family but not to another. The manager of a local nursery offered these tips for checking that a nursery has the right kind of ethos.

- Look to see that the environment is stimulating, rather than the teacher, or carer, as they may not be there all the time
- Are there plenty of things to touch?
- Is the equipment treated with care by everyone?
- Is there free access to pencils, paper, and other safe materials?
- Are the staff happy? Do they smile at you, and your children?

Variety of carers

SOME PARENTS prefer to be their child's prime carer, and for the child to see it like that. This means that the idea of a childminder, or a nanny, is not as appealing as a nursery, where of course there would be continuity of carers, but not just one person, 'mother figure', in the child's life.

DISADVANTAGES OF THE NURSERY OR CRECHE

Hours

ALTHOUGH THEY'RE better, they're still not as flexible as other forms of childcare. You have to drop your child after the nursery is open, and pick him up before it has shut. If those hours don't suit you, then there are no alternatives, apart from trying another nursery or opting for a different form of care.

Not for all children

SOME PARENTS feel that the nursery atmosphere is not for their child. It is a busy active place, which the more timid children might find too much. Amy sends her children to nursery, but not until they are two, because she feels they belong at home until then. *'I do think that babies are better off at home until they are two, so they have a familiar environment all the time.'*

Competition

THERE IS a school of thought that feels that children in a nursery have to compete for attention more than they would in a home environment. The question is, is that a bad thing, if indeed it is the case?

Cost

NURSERY CARE is one of the more expensive childcare options. There don't seem to be reductions if you have more than one child there.

Booking your place

NURSERIES IN many areas are oversubscribed. This means that it can be more difficult to find part-time places, and places for babies are particularly popular. You may need to book your child's place there a long time in advance, for example, as soon as you find out you are pregnant. Sometimes this is a lot to think about when so much else is going on in your life.

Commitment

As in any other business, there needs to be an element of organisation. You are likely to be asked to commit yourself, probably financially, and in advance, for your child's place. Some nurseries also expect you to take the same four weeks' holiday a year that they close in, or else pay for your place even though you are away.

CHOICES AND CHILDREN

There is no specific choice that will fit all children, or even some who fit into one grouping. Different families have different needs and it depends on all sorts on variables, such as:

- Economics
- Child's personality
- Child's preferences
- Parents' preferences
- Number of children in family.

Karen, who is the manager of three day nurseries in the Home Counties, spoke about her views on the nursery as a form of childcare: *'I feel that the ethos of a good nursery is that it is child-centred, and runs at the child's pace. Our nurseries focus on the children, there are no household chores to be done. We take them to the park, to the local shops, to post letters. We try to make them feel part of the local community.*

Nursery gives children the extended family again. Being at home with mother for five years is just not enough, children need extra stimulation, they are happier with other friends than with adults. And if they have enough equipment to play with, they don't fight.

Also, the staff are happy because they have the support and companionship of their colleagues; they aren't isolated as a mother or a nanny could be.

There is a down side of course, you must still pay if your child is ill; you must still pay if you take holidays outside the four weeks that the nursery closes; it can become institutional, as we have to have rules.'

Karen had been a primary school teacher before she set up her nurseries. She felt that children were arriving at school without reaching their potential. *'Children are absorbent during those pre-school years and need stimulation. They learn from other children rather than adults, so we need to give them access to what they need to learn from.'*

Karen has a flexible approach to getting children settled into nursery. She finds that the younger they start, the sooner they adjust to life there: *'The difficult stage tends to be from two to three, but if they won't settle and their mother wants to stay, then that's fine. Sometimes having the parent stay just once gives the child more confidence.*

When a child isn't settled here, we would take them to watch a video, or take them for a walk in the pushchair — it really depends on what normally happens to them in their own home.

If a child is upset, it's important to distract them — it gives them the opportunity to switch off, and save face, if they're having a tantrum.

We don't have a typical day as such, but there are certain key aspects, such as making sure the equipment is circulated so that everyone gets a turn, and making sure everything is out for them to play with. They also have a rest after lunch, so before they come to us we try to encourage parents to get them into a similar routine with their rest at the same time.'

Pat was able to make use of her company's workplace crèche and comments: *'I always intended to return to work, unless there was something wrong with my baby. Happily, he was perfect, so I went back when he was four months old. My company was going through a period of transition, which included relocation. The relocation was closer to home, but until that happened, my mother took Sean three days a week.*

The brand new workplace crèche was being built off-site and it was brilliant – it was another thing that encouraged me to come back to work. It was close by in case of any problems, they provided good food, there was a large garden for him to play in.'

Laura's daughter, Holly, changed from going to a childminder to a workplace crèche when she was two and a half: *'My children started going to the office crèche when Holly was two and a half and Anna six months.*

Holly, having been to a childminder for two years, found the change difficult. She was okay if she was kept busy and of course the crèche is a stimulating environment, but there were times when she was clingy and aggressive, which was rather worrying. I was unhappy about the situation but having made the decision, I felt I wanted to see it through.

Even though it was difficult for her, I felt that the crèche was the right thing. I had faith in my employer that it was a good crèche, and I had contact with the other parents, and I got a lot of positive feedback from them.'

Holly did settle there shortly afterwards and has now started school. Laura says: *'Holly was in the crèche for four days a week over two years. She went into school very easily, which I think was due to the crèche. She is not daunted by large numbers of children.'*

Julia's daughter Beth had started off with a childminder, but had to make a transition from childminder to part-time nursery place. Julia explains: *'I arranged to go into work late for a month to give Beth time to get used to the nursery for two days a week, while she still went to Anne for the other days. It was traumatic dropping her off because she didn't want to go in. She hated it – she would scream and hang on to me. She hated her routine being changed and would say in the car, "Where am I going today?" It got to the point where she was physically sick when she got there. How am I going to cope with this, I asked myself.*

So I asked Anne if she would take her for the hour before nursery and then on to the nursery. She was happy to. In fact, when Anne took her, she was fine. Then we had a three-week holiday, and when we came back, Anne was away. I had to take Beth for a week, and we were back to square one. I did think she was genuinely distressed, but I tried very hard not to be seen to be wound up by it.

The next week, when Anne was back, Beth was very upset again. That upset Anne, who offered to have her back full time, but I felt that I didn't want to change the routine again. I had given up her place at playgroup, and felt she should be mixing with other children. It wasn't the answer for Anne to have her back full time. Anyway, it didn't take long before she settled, but it was definitely the worst time.'

THE VIEW FROM THE NURSERY

REBECCA WORKS in a nursery, as a nursery nurse. She's been qualified for about a year, and particularly likes working with the babies. She gives us a taste of what it is like to spend a day in the nursery: *'There are about 120 children and babies enrolled in the nursery, but only about 40 or 50 of them are full time. The nursery is open from 7am till 7pm, but not many of the children are here for that long: a full-time place for a baby is £123 a week.*

What I like about it is the atmosphere and the company. If I was a nanny in a private home, I think I'd get bored, and would miss having people to chat to during my work.

If the babies start coming when they're under three months, they tend to settle very well, before they've got used to any other routine. If they come at around four to six months, they sometimes cry when they are left, but what we see and what the parents see is very different. Most babies stop crying very shortly after the parent has gone. Once they're distracted, they stop. Very few carry on crying and don't adjust, but it does occasionally happen. I used to see one mother drop off her little boy, who was five months old. He would cry, so she would leave and sit and cry in the car park.

I try to distract them as quickly as possible. I don't want parents to feel guilty. I can imagine how it feels. It must really hurt. My job is to do my best for the children and the parents. I need to have a good relationship with them.

Generally, it can take one to two weeks for a baby to adjust. Often it's only the separation point that is difficult, but some get upset when other parents pick up their children.

Some are fine at first, but as they get older they get more upset. Really it's better if the parent leaves as soon as possible. If they leave quickly and wait outside the door they can hear that the baby is settled. It only takes a few minutes to divert them.

I feel that children thrive on a nursery atmosphere. They are able to play

all day, rather than waiting for a mother to play when she can, but like everything else, it helps if the child is prepared for the change.

We have a loose structure to the day, but being in the baby room, they can
drop off to sleep at any time. I can only remember one time when all the babies
were asleep at the same time.

When they come in they have some breakfast, then they sleep or play. At
about ten, we do nappy changes all round. Then there's more sleep or play,
and around 11.45am we tidy away for lunch. Sometimes we take them out
to the playground, and there is a separate hall if it's raining. The older children go outside for outings and nature walks. We try to stick to the parents'
routine as much as possible.

At our nursery, you can bring your child in for two trial mornings. On the
first one, the parent stays, and at the other one the parent goes. That way,
everyone knows what to expect, and people get to know faces.

I do get attached to the children even though I shouldn't. But it's not surprising because you have to like babies to do this job. What I really enjoy is seeing the babies developing – doing things for the first time. Not only do we get fond of the babies, but they get fond of us too. I haven't met any yet that I didn't like.'

Lisa is the assistant manager in a small nursery. She said that more and more people want childcare for their babies from three months and there is a long waiting list for places: *'The younger the baby is, the easier it is for us to settle them, but then it gets easier when they are older if they have already been to a playgroup or are used to socialising with other children, preferably without their mums. Most children do settle. I've been here for two and a half years and there has only been one that couldn't make the adjustment. Sometimes a child just isn't ready, but if you can wait a month or two, it can make all the difference.*

Nurseries need routines. You can't run any institution without it. This means that a child will learn the importance of rules very young – too young for some. But on the other hand, we try to give a good balance of play and structure, and it makes the transition to the rules of school that much easier.

Our day is a combination of free play, discussion time, talking about the weather, breaks for food and drinks, visits to the post office, the park (we have triple buggies), and structured play. We also have a play area outside.'

WHAT SHOULD YOU LOOK FOR WHEN CHOOSING A NURSERY?

- Plenty of qualified staff
- Signs of staff playing with the children
- Ask for their policies on discipline and behaviour
- Lots of good, well used equipment
- Signs that the children relate well to the staff
- Signs of lots of free time so they can learn to play with other children
- Ask to see registration certificate and make sure it is current.

Louise has nothing but praise for the nursery her son went to. He was her first child, and one of the advantages for her was that he had plenty of company during the day: *'Luke went to nursery from nine months to*

20 months. He was a happy-go-lucky child, so he settled easily, and since he was an only child at the time, I liked him playing with others when I was at work.

He was able to do things like painting and messy games that he probably wouldn't have done so young if he had been at home, but they are equipped to be able to do this, which I liked. You also know that they are going to be playing, rather than watching too much television.'

FINDING A NURSERY

THE BEST way is probably a word-of-mouth recommendation, but, under the Children Act, all nurseries, including private ones, must be registered with Social Services, so you can apply to them for information. The condition of the premises, staff qualification, staff to baby or child ratio, are all governed by the Act.

CHAPTER *eight* Nannies

A NUMBER OF parents prefer to choose childcare that means their children can stay in their own home – they choose from: a live-in or out nanny, a mother's help, an au pair or even a childminder who prefers to go to the child's house.

A NANNY

HAVING A NANNY is no longer the sole privilege of the rich, but is becoming one of the most popular forms of childcare, along with having an au pair, which is discussed in Chapter Nine.

There are lots of different types of nanny, ranging from the elite, traditional nannies, to a newly qualified nanny of 19. A nanny who does not have a qualification would be expected to have extensive experience. But the choice is yours, of course. You may find some-one, probably through word of mouth, who has no formal qualifica-tions or work experience, but is a natural with children.

A nanny is unlikely to do any domestic work; her job is to look after the children, on a sole charge basis, which means that she takes responsibility while she is on duty. Many nannies do not like their employers to be around because it sometimes creates confusion about who is in charge. It's quite difficult for a mother to ignore her child crying, and she may feel she wants to intervene, but really it is for the nanny to deal with an issue, so that there is no question of her being undermined in the eyes of the child.

Nannies may live in or outside the home. If she lives in, she is like-ly to cost less in terms of salary, because she will also be receiving her board and lodging, which would be part of the package – you can't charge rent. This means one thing – you must have a home that is big enough to accommodate an extra person. She will need her own room, at least, which is big enough for her to be comfortable in during her time off.

She may well need the use of a car, if she doesn't have one of her own, to ferry the children around to friends and mother and toddler groups. This would apply whether she lives in or out.

Cost

THIS DEPENDS on a number of variables, such as age, experience and location. It ranges from about £100–£250+ per week (these are net salaries). If you employ a nanny, expect to pay tax and National Insurance on her salary, so remember this when budgeting. Alternatively, there are now firms who run a payroll system for nannies, taking all the calculating and declaring out of your hands.

Nanny agencies will supply you with likely costs in your area. *The Lady* is always full of adverts and there is also your local *Yellow Pages*.

ADVANTAGES OF THE LIVE-IN NANNY

All in a warm, family relationship

WHEN A NANNY is living in the home, she could be treated either as an employee, or part of the family. That is something that every family will decide for themselves, but one of the advantages of the live-in nanny is that she is part of the family home and will get to know all members of the family. She is there all the time for the child, who will see her as part of the family and enjoy the security that gives.

Staying in own home

THIS CAN increase a child's sense of security and it may help to reduce the number of colds, coughs and other bugs that children being cared for outside the family home often suffer from.

Nannies are often employed by working parents who have a fair amount of commuting to do – it may be that they are out of the house from seven in the morning to seven at night, so the benefits of the child being at home during that time are obvious.

A more relaxed start to the day

THIS ASPECT of having a nanny is a real winner. If the nanny is in the home, it also means that she can't be late for work. She is there, on the spot, and often will be expected to start work at seven or eight o'clock, leaving you to worry about getting yourself ready without having to get the children washed, dressed and breakfasted too.

Another angle to this is that it means you can spend more time with the children at leisure. If you're all rushing to get out of the door by a certain time, there is only a remote likelihood of talking to the children, or cuddling the baby, in the morning. If you have a nanny to take over from you, it means you can prepare yourself, and maybe sit down to breakfast with the children before you set off, leaving the nanny to get them washed and dressed after you have gone.

Babysitting services

WHEN YOU negotiate terms with a nanny, it wouldn't be unreasonable to expect her to babysit as part of her duties; say, one or two evenings a week. You may have to pay her extra for more evenings than that.

This means that as your babysitter is someone who knows your children well, it is one less person to find at short notice. It also means that she can put the children to bed, which is a great bonus. Very often, parents feel they have to get the children tucked up in bed and asleep before they can go out, and pray that they don't wake before they come back. Having a nanny on hand for this service is likely to ease the burden considerably.

Cost effective with more children

YOU MAY pay a nanny more if you have more than one child, but, unlike for a nursery, it won't be double. In fact, the more children you have, the more cost effective having a nanny is likely to be.

Variety

IF EXPERIENCE is an important criterion then you may choose an older nanny, but you may want someone who is young and energetic, who wants to take the children swimming or to the playground. A young, single nanny may be a good idea, not only for the child but also for you and your privacy, as she will probably have an active social life and want to be out for a lot of her spare time.

Some help around the house

ALTHOUGH NANNIES would not expect to be asked to do general housework, they could be expected to be responsible for all care to do with the children, such as:

- Wash and iron the children's clothes
- Keep the children's rooms tidy
- Plan, buy and prepare the children's food.

One-to-one relationship with the children

YOUR CHILDREN will probably form a strong relationship with their nanny. They will miss out on having other children about, but they will, on the other hand, have someone's undivided attention, rather

than having to compete for attention with a larger group of children. This is very much substitute parenting, and may not appeal to parents who feel that it is good for children to become more independent and learn to share. It is worth remembering that even if you employ a nanny you can still send your children to playgroups, toddler groups and mother and baby clubs – only it will be the nanny, not you, who fetches and carries.

DISADVANTAGES OF THE LIVE-IN NANNY

Personality clashes

THIS IS more likely to happen if someone is coming into your home every day. It is possible that things will seem to be going well, but then you won't see eye to eye on something and a rift will develop. It goes without saying that you need to think very carefully about this when you interview your candidates. Try to find out as much as possible about their habits and preferences.

If there is a personality clash, it's worth talking about it as soon as possible, otherwise an awkward situation can rapidly become an untenable one. Being direct and pleasant is important, and all of your diplomatic skills will be needed, but unless you feel there is a fundamental problem, it is worth negotiating a solution rather than risk losing your carer and possibly a very good companion for the child.

There all the time

WHILST IN many ways it is great to have someone available, and around all the time, it can also be an imposition on your private life. It may take a bit of getting used to, and it is certainly one of the factors to weigh up when deciding on whether you want someone to live in.

Abuse of hospitality

AGAIN, THIS is a sensitive issue: where is the line drawn between making yourself at home, and clearing the cupboard out of peanuts/chocolates/white wine week after week, or spending most of your spare time on the telephone? Ground rules need to be established at the outset.

Missing out on the experience of own children

A YOUNG nanny is unlikely to have had children of her own. Some parents find this to be a disadvantage because they feel that, valuable though the childcare courses are, there is no substitute for the real thing and the experience that it gives you. A nanny may not under-stand what it is like to leave your child for the first time, whereas a childminder can more easily empathise with you.

Fast turnover

NANNIES TEND to move on to different jobs on a regular basis. Not all of them, and not every three months, but there is a tendency for them to move maybe after a year or eighteen months. This is probably due to their relative youth, where they want to go on to new things or different areas. It is a good idea to talk about this before you employ someone – you could make it clear that you expect a minimum stay of eighteen months. Although it's unlikely to be enforceable, it will give your nanny a chance to decide if that is what she wants, and hopefully she will try to meet your needs as well as her own.

The trouble with the faster turnover is that your child may have formed an attachment, and then you have to start all over again.

What's going on while you're out?

SOME PARENTS just don't like there to be someone in their house when they are not there. Although the house may be tidy at the end of the day when you come home, you have no way of knowing what state it has been in during the day, unless you unexpectedly call in . . . but that would indicate a lack of trust. Trust is the key ingredient in all types of childcare – but particularly when you have a relative stranger in your home.

Bigger bills

A DIRECT consequence of your nanny and child being at home all day is bigger household bills; the heating will need to be on during the colder weather, not forgetting lighting, telephone and so on.

Is the house big enough?

THIS OPTION is not available to anyone who doesn't have a spare room, which has to be bigger than a boxroom, to allow your nanny to make it comfortable and a relaxing place to be when she is off-duty. Not only that, she may not want to stay cooped up in one room when she isn't working. You need to think about the general space in your house – is there enough for all of you to be comfortable?

A stranger in the home

BEFORE SHE has settled in, it may well seem that your new nanny is a stranger to you and you will have to take a certain amount on trust. Nannies are not registered, police vetted or approved unless you employ a nanny straight from college, as all students starting childcare courses are police vetted and approved. Hopefully you will feel that you have made all reasonable checks on her, but there can sometimes be a period during which you aren't quite sure. It's just getting used to having someone else around, and wondering whether they may be the nosey type or clumsy, or not bother to clean the bath out.

Flexibility

YOU MAY find that some nannies are less than flexible when it comes to anything to do with running the house. Quite definitely, they are not there to be cleaners, but there is a difference between expecting them to do the hoovering every day, and knowing that they won't mind washing up a few coffee cups, or bringing in the washing when it starts to rain.

DAILY NANNY

A NANNY WHO doesn't live in will be doing exactly the same job, but will come in to your house every day to do it. She is, therefore, likely to live locally. It costs a little more in terms of salary, but may turn out cheaper overall, if you take things like use of the phone, and food, into account.

Caitlin has had the same nanny for all three of her children, but she has never lived in. *'Maria was our next door neighbour in our last house. She had done some nannying when she was younger. At first, the children went in to her, but when number three came along, Maria wanted to look after them in our home. I think that was because she can leave them and the mess here at the end of the day. Now we've moved, so Maria comes over here when I need her.*

I pay her on an hourly, rather than a weekly rate, as she is part time. For three children, she is paid £5 an hour. When the eldest starts school, I expect I will drop her hourly rate as she'll only have two again. It works out cheaper for me to have her than to send them all to nursery, which is about £20 a day, per child.

I have total confidence in Maria. Fortunately we are similar sorts of people, both tidy, so she leaves the house as we would both want to find it. We have a good relationship, as she does with the children: they love her and she loves them.

Although she doesn't have to help around the house, I often find that she's put the washing out when I come home.

In spite of all that, though, I am the one who takes overall responsibility for the children, mainly because Maria doesn't have a car. So although she can walk Rosie to school and pick her up, if she was sick and needed picking up quickly, it would be my responsibility.'

THE NANNY FROM HELL

EVERYBODY HAS a friend of a friend who has had an experience of the nanny from hell, but fortunately they are few and far between.

Sarah was looking for a nanny for her little girl when she was going back to work part time: *'This girl came from an agency, so she should have been vetted by them. I was going back to work for two days a week, so she came in before I started and there was no problem at all. I was around the house, and I could even hear her on the baby listener at times and I had no reason to think there would be any problem.*

But when I went back to work, everything changed. I would get back and the place was in a real mess. She'd had her friends over to lunch, which I didn't mind – but she was using our food, and our best dinner service, which she put in the dishwasher afterwards.

If this was a one-off, I could have over-looked it, but she'd only just started with us, and she was doing it regularly.

Then one day, Emily had a cold and I decided to work from home. The nanny completely lost her temper. She said that she had already made arrangements and I was taking over – she really went mad at me, so there was an enormous row. That was the end of the arrangement.

It made me feel very guilty that I had left Emily with her, but she seemed very happy to be with her. I had no reason to think otherwise. I also learnt from my friends afterwards that she gave them reason to think she wasn't a good carer at toddler group, but nobody told me at the time. I was quite cross about that. I wish they'd told me.

It's embarrassing now because she lives locally and I see her around. The whole thing was a really unfortunate experience.'

CHECKING

Checking methods you might consider:

- Ask your friends to drop in and check on a new nanny
- Ask the nanny to go to the same toddler groups as your friends
- Follow up references independently of the agency
- Draw up a contract between you
- Discuss what are acceptable limits of behaviour and include them in the contract.

Sarah suggests that parents should, *'Follow your instincts. We felt that we had done as much as we could: we had seen her frequently beforehand, and I had been around when she first started. Nigel and I felt that something wasn't right, not a strong feeling, but there all the same. But as Emily was happy, we felt that was paramount. So what if we didn't like her. But looking back on it, Emily was only two and a half. Not really old enough to know that what the nanny was doing was wrong – maybe she actually enjoyed all the socialising, who knows?'*

FORTUNATELY, not everyone's experience of nannies is like Sarah's.

Amy has four children, and has had three nannies, who have both lived in and out. *'Our first live-in nanny came to us when my second child was fourteen weeks old. She came for seven months, then got homesick and went back to the West Country.*

Our second came from New Zealand. We hadn't met her until she arrived in the country, so it was a bit of a risk, but she was suggested to us by a friend, and we were getting desperate. We took it to be fate that someone asked us if we needed anyone at that point. But on top of that, to be honest we had little choice.

She stayed with us for eighteen months, and it was a very stable period. She wanted to move on after that, not because she didn't like it, but because the time had come for her to move on. You have to accept that that is the case with many nannies. Both sides were happy when she left.

When I look back, I think we tried too hard with the first nanny. Now we feel that they either will like you or they won't. They have got to fit in with your family.

Now we have a daily nanny. She's the youngest of them all, she has no qualifications and she is by far the best. She has a way with children. We got her because she is the daughter of a friend.'

Amy thinks that childcare arrangements vary tremendously according to the size and age of your family. Whilst a nursery can be good for one phase, it isn't necessarily right for all — and of course, children vary in what is best suited to them. She doesn't like her children to be cared for out of the house until they are over two years old — 'the best place to have them cared for is at home, so that even if you're not there, they don't have to cope with too much change, and have the security of the same place all the time.'

Now that her children are getting older (but they're all under five), she feels she's got past the need for live-in care. 'But I didn't have any problems with live-in nannies. We were worried at the outset about her sitting in between us on the sofa, but she would go off and bath in the evenings.

If you want privacy, you have to think about the sort of room she is living in. Is there a television? We also put a phone extension in her room.

The only way I get out in the morning is that the nanny comes in at eight o'clock. I leave at 9.15am so there is an overlap, where I can get myself ready. We all know what we are aiming at.'

NANNY SHARE

IF TAKING ON a nanny is beyond your budget, or if you are only going back part time, then a nanny share may be the answer for you. Diana used a nanny share arrangement: 'My son Sean was about ten months old. I wanted to work part time, I wanted him to be looked after at home, but

I couldn't afford to pay a full-time nanny. He had been going to a childmin-
der, but it was such a lot of hassle: I'm not very organised, and my work was
unpredictable. I really needed the extra flexibility that a nanny could give. So
first of all I advertised in the local NCT newsletter for the sharer, and found
a GP who was pregnant and wanted to work for half the week. Then we
found the nanny.

We both had two and a half days each — our change-over day was
Thursday. We also had the option of doubling up if something else came up

on another day, but neither of us wanted the nanny to have both the children all of the time.

Sean adjusted very well to the arrangement. I used to work upstairs, so he hardly noticed whether I was there or not, as he had his own toys and his own surroundings. It was more difficult as he got older. When he was about three, he got confused about which day was a mummy day and which was a nanny day. I think that was partly because my days were spread out. Really I think it is better to have your time in a block, so there is less confusion.

The other down side of having a Monday as one of your days is that you miss out on Bank Holidays. Because I was doing the sort of job that if I wasn't working, I wasn't earning, these days made a difference to me. We solved it by doubling up on the Tuesday after a Bank Holiday.

I didn't find it difficult to work from home, because I knew that the minute Sally came through the door I was paying her. That was a pretty good incentive to get on with work. What I did find hard was missing out on doing some things with Sean. For example, his music group was on a Monday, so it was always Sally who took him.

Sean and Sally didn't have a problem about not disturbing me when I was working, but other people don't understand that you are working as much as anyone who's in an office, and they would drop round for a coffee. But Sally used to answer the door when I was working and the penny dropped soon after that.

This arrangement worked very well for us – Sally stayed with us for seven years, and the GP and I both went on to have second children who she looked after too. The two sets of children became great friends, and one thing I think that made it work so well was that on Thursdays (changeover day) we all had lunch together: Sally, the mums and the children. This meant that we communicated well, and that Sally wasn't expected to bear messages between the two of us. I think that did a lot for the relationship with Sally.

Looking back, I don't think we looked at illness and holidays seriously enough. We had a contract that was signed by us all, and we (the mothers) wanted six weeks' holiday, so we gave Sally six weeks too. But we didn't say she had to make her holidays coincide with ours, so she effectively had twelve weeks off that year. The following year we amended the contract so that she had to take four of the six weeks when we had ours.

We also went through a stage where Sally was sick a lot and I think we should have put a condition in the contract that we would pay her for so long, and after that she would only be eligible for statutory sick pay. Once we had

*started to pay her, it was very difficult to stop, but with a clause in your con-
tract, there is less embarrassment about it.*

*The arrangement worked very well for us. The lunches helped to keep it
running smoothly, and you have to keep working at it and adapting it. But
Sally was an important part of our life. The arrangement only stopped because
I wanted to work for longer hours and she got married and wanted to start a
family, but we're still in touch.'*

A nanny share that involves the child being cared for outside their
home may need to be registered. Check with your local authority.

FINDING A NANNY

THERE ARE A number of routes for this. They are:

- Word of mouth, contacts, friends
- Nanny/au pair agencies
- Advertising: in local newspaper; in any job seeker-type paper;
  in *The Lady*, which is a well-known magazine forum for placing nannies or au pairs.

IF YOU GO through an agency, they can do the initial selection work
for you, identifying those on their books who meet your criteria. They
would then be able to give you a shortlist of more suitable candidates.

If you don't want to use an agency, then your advert is likely to bring
you a response of more and less suitable applicants, which you will need
to hone down into a reasonable number of first interview applicants.

TELEPHONE INTERVIEWING

IT MAY BE that you want to talk to applicants who have responded to
your advert over the phone, to get further details and to find out who
are the strongest candidates and interview them first.

Think about your key criteria and work out some questions that
will elicit useful answers.

MAKE SURE that you tell the applicant when you will contact her
again. If she's not on the shortlist, you should let her know as soon as

NANNY APPLICATION QUESTIONS

Full name _____ Telephone number _____

Full address _____ Age _____

Smoker? YES/NO   Earliest start date _____
Total years working with children _____

Previous experience:
1. Number of children _____ 2. Number of children _____ 3. Number of children _____

   Length of job _____ Length of job _____ Length of job _____

Other details _____

Qualifications _____

GCSEs _____

A-Levels/other _____

Own car? Yes/No   Can drive? Yes/No

If no, how would get to work? _____

References

1. Personal ref _____ 2. Professional refs (to be brought to interview)

Can I contact refs by phone? _____

Current income _____

Pay _____ Other benefits _____ Hours _____

Current duties _____

Want to interview? Yes/No

If yes, date _____

     time _____

possible, either by phone, or by dropping her a note. If you're not sure, say so. It's better to be direct and open than to fudge the issue so that the candidate is misled.

INTERVIEWING FACE TO FACE

THINK ABOUT where you will interview – you both need to be comfortable. What about your child, or children? Naturally, you will want them to meet the nanny, but maybe you don't want to be interrupted throughout the interview. It may be worth having another person there who can take them into the garden when you want to concentrate on the nanny. If you have a partner, it could be beneficial for both of you if he is there – it gives you a second opinion for discussion later on.

Plan the interview

YOU NEED to come away after having done more than have a chat. Write down a job specification – and a copy for the candidate.

Make sure you have read their CV before the interview. Nothing is more galling for a candidate than to be asked questions that make it clear that you haven't read it properly. Remember, she is judging you, too, and making a decision about whether she wants to work with you.

Make a list of the questions that you want answering, and think about how relevant that list is to the job spec.

Put the candidate at ease

THINK OF an ice breaker. Maybe you can find something on her CV to open with, or why she chose to work with children.

Make sure there will be no interruptions. Hopefully the children are organised, but make sure the phone is off the hook, or the answerphone is on. If you have friends who tend to drop by, warn them that this is Interview Day.

Be open, fair and honest – the interview is a two-way process. They are there to find out about you, as well as the job. Don't assume that they will want the job.

INTERVIEW

Name:

Training:

Any formal qualifications?
Are the certificates available? Yes/No
Any other qualifications?
Where was the training?
What was the training like?
Why are you a nanny?

Experience:

How many previous jobs?
How many children (including age and sex)
How long did each job last? What were
the reasons for leaving each job?
How much was sole charge?

References:

Available? Yes/No
Can I contact referees directly?

Home and background:

Where do you live?
What do your parents do?
How do you get on with your parents?
Any other close family?
Do you have any children?
Do you get homesick?

Boyfriends:

Do you have one?
Where does he live?
How serious is it?

Other details:

Do you smoke? Yes/No
Do you drive? Yes/No
Clean licence?
Do you own a car?
Religious?
What hobbies do you have?

Local knowledge:

Do you know the area?
Do you have family and friends nearby?

Health:

Overall level of fitness
Any recurring illnesses?
Major operations?

Children:

Any preferences in terms of age/sex?
How would you entertain the children?
What are your views on discipline?

Sole charge:

What are your feelings about it?
How do you feel about responsibility?
What about dangers in the house? (ask
questions on common emergencies.)

The future:

What are your ambitions?
Where do you see yourself in two to five
years?
How long do you see yourself staying with us?

Listen to them

IT IS a common mistake when interviewing for the client to spend too much time talking. It's easy to talk for ages about your children, particularly with a potential nanny, but that's not the purpose of the interview.

You should spend 80% of the time listening and 20% talking.

Ask open questions

AN OPEN question is one that encourages a more detailed response than 'yes' or 'no'. For example, you could ask: 'Do you enjoy playing with babies?' or you could say, 'What do you like about spending time with a baby?'

The second question will elicit a fuller response than the first, to which she is bound to reply in the affirmative. You will get more clues to a person's identity by trying to find as many open questions as possible to ask her, and let her talk.

Another example would be: 'My child is a fussy eater. Will you be able to deal with that?' It may be better to ask, 'Tell me about working with different children, where it hasn't been plain sailing'.

Beware of prejudging

YOU COULD lose out on the best candidate by rejecting her because of an immediate reaction to her appearance. I know a nanny, who is covered in tattoos, and she might cause a sharp intake of breath when she appears at first. But she is excellent at her job. It would be easy to prejudge her, but the employer would be missing out.

Ending the interview

AGREE AN action. Say how many people you will be interviewing and if you can't contact them for a week, then say so. Try to get some idea of her level of interest – it may be useful to you when making a decision.

Make sure you don't forget to take her references

CHECK THAT they are recent – and if not, why not? Check that you can ring people to talk to them about her. This is vital for your own security.

Plan to take about an hour

BY THE time you have explained the duties, and have wound up at the end, it doesn't leave all that much time for asking questions – therefore, keep them succinct.

Some people find it very useful, if they are interviewing a lot of people, to take a Polaroid photo of the candidates to use as an *aide-mémoire*. If you do so, make sure that the candidate is quite happy with this.

It's probably best not to arrange more than three interviews in any day.

On the page 116 is Alex's sample interview sheet, which is useful for looking at the types of questions you might want to ask.

This is only one person's set of questions. It may differ from the ones that you think are important, but equally it may give you some ideas and prompts. It is worth preparing something like this in advance: it gives you something to work from, and may stop you forgetting to ask something vital. Note-taking is something else you may find useful – as this is likely to be quite an informal interview, it shouldn't pose any problem. Your candidate may well want to take notes too.

CONTRACTS

ONCE you have chosen a nanny, be clear about duties and responsibilities, salary, holidays, and so on. Having this written down in one document, agreed by all parties, is a very good way of resolving any disputes or misunderstandings at a later date. You can make a contract up for yourself, and both parties then sign it to say that they agree to it. A contract is enforceable by law, so long as it doesn't overrule any legislation, which would make it void. So, for example, if you made a contract with a childminder, in which it stated that she would have four of your children under five, where the Children Act says she can't have more than three under-fives, then the existing law over-rules your contract and makes it void.

You can make a verbal contract, which theoretically is enforceable by law, but would be much more difficult to prove than a written contract. Having a document to refer to is a practicality which helps all parties know what is expected of them.

On the next page is a sample contract which one mother used with her nanny.

THIS CONTRACT lays out clearly the nature of the employment. Not every contract has to be as detailed, but it may be helpful for both parties when employing a nanny. Other carers, such as au pairs, mother's helps, are self-employed, therefore, although you may prefer some sort of contract, it does not have to be so detailed.

A final word from a mother who chose her nanny from an interview: *'First of all, I got on well with her. She brought her CV with her, which appealed to my sense of order. She had previously worked as a volunteer with children, which indicated to me that she liked being with them. She had had a good education, which was important to me. When I asked her what she might do with the children during the day, she had similar ideas to mine. The questions that she asked me were very revealing too: she wanted to know my views on discipline, and she wanted to know what would happen if we disagreed on an issue like that. It seemed to me that she was committed and interested, and I've been proved right. We are very happy with her.'*

SAMPLE OF A CONTRACT OF EMPLOYMENT

Employer's name _____

_____

Employee's name _____

_____

NI number _____

Employment will begin on _____

Responsibilities:

Job title: Nanny
Basic hours: Monday – Friday,
7.45am – 6pm

Extra hours:

One evening per week babysitting is
required. Time off will be given in lieu
of babysitting (normally Wednesday
morning till 11am)

Any extra babysitting will be paid at a
rate of £____ per hour.

Duties:
– provide supervised daily care for children;
– plan, buy materials for, prepare and
  give three daily meals (one hot) to
  children;
– encourage physical and intellectual
  development of children;

– organise and undertake any visits to
  doctors, dentists (always advise
  mother beforehand, except in an
  emergency, when you first attend to
  the child's needs and contact either
  parent as soon as possible);
– plan and organise daily/weekly
  schedules to include current activities, such as nursery, plus a mix of
  outdoor and indoor activities;
– wash and iron children's clothes;
– keep children's room tidy;
– wash and iron children's bedding
  weekly;
– shop for all necessary clothes and
  other child/baby items, eg nappies;
– ensure no one smokes in the house or
  brings animals into the house;
– tidy up toys and after meals every day.

Remuneration
Salary: £____ per week, paid weekly in
arrears, net of National Insurance and
Income Tax, which will be paid by Mr
and Mrs C–. A salary review will take
place annually.
Holidays: 20 days per annum, plus all
public holidays. You are entitled to
choose two weeks' holiday each year,
for which notice is required (it would
be appreciated if this was taken at a
mutually convenient time). The
remaining holiday should be taken at
the same time as your employers.

CONTRACT OF EMPLOYMENT

Car

You will have use of a car, plus all petrol when on duty. Please inform when petrol is required. If you use your own car to carry out duties, a mileage allowance of ___p per mile is payable.

Telephone use

Itemised calls which do not exceed £___ per quarter will be allowed.

Refreshments

All refreshments whilst on duty for yourself, and a reasonable number of other nannies and their charges are included.

Sick pay

You are entitled to statutory sick pay (100% of salary for up to two weeks per annum). Any illness that prevents you from coming to work should be notified to us as soon as possible, and no later than 7am on the day in question so that alternative arrangements can be made.

Pension

We do not run a pension scheme.

Confidentiality

It is a condition of employment that now and at all times in the future (except where legally required) the employee should keep the affairs and concerns of the household, and its transactions and business, confidential.

Disciplinary action

Reasons which may give cause for disciplinary measures include:

1. Job incompetence
2. Unreliable timekeeping
3. Failure to comply with instructions
4. Conduct during or after hours prejudicial to the family.

In such an event, disciplinary action will proceed as follows:

1. First verbal warning
2. Second verbal warning
3. Dismissal with four weeks' notice.

The following actions would lead to immediate dismissal:

1. Theft
2. Substance abuse (including drunkenness)
3. Child abuse
4. Acting unsafely with children.

Termination:

In the first four weeks of employment one week's notice is required by either side. After four weeks' continuous service either side may terminate employment by giving six weeks' notice.

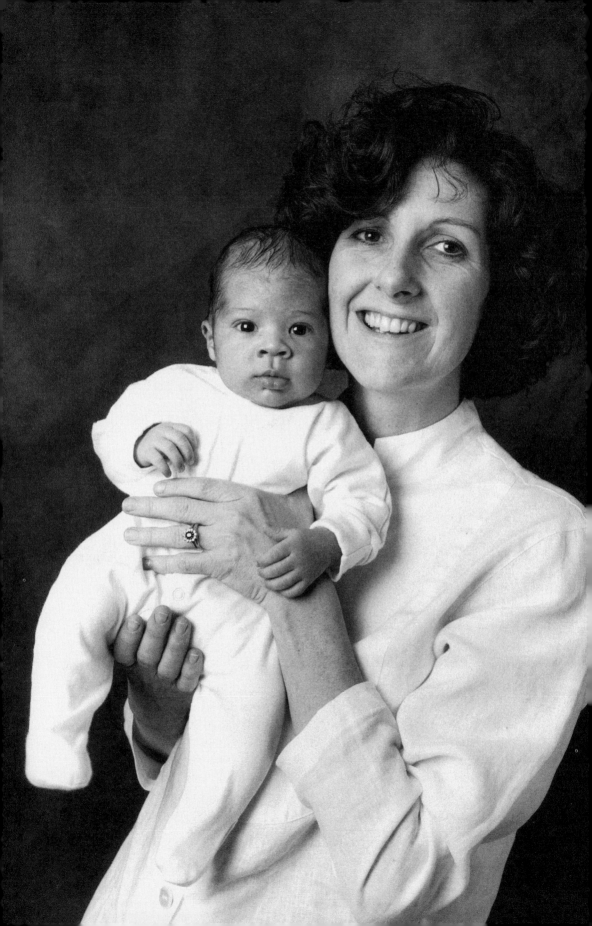

CHAPTER *nine* *Au pairs and other support*

NANNIES TEND to fulfil a more long-term need and usually bring with them experience and a desire to blend in with the family. Other carers who look after your child at your home may only do so for a short period of time, or may take on the job as a route to another goal. A maternity nurse and a mother's help are good examples of the former, and au pairs usually want to learn or improve their English.

MATERNITY NURSES

THESE NURSES are either highly qualified or very, very experienced. They can command a net salary of up to £200 or £300 per week – a cost that may be out of the reach of many people. You need to book one from the moment you know that you are pregnant, because they are very much in demand. The disadvantage is that you have to book them from a particular date, but if your baby is late, you may lose the nurse, since they may well have another baby booked.

The basic idea is that they get the baby into a routine for you, so that by the time the maternity nurse leaves, the baby is more predictable. She will sleep with the baby in the nursery and if the mother is breastfeeding, she will only bring the baby in to her for feeds.

The maternity nurse appeals to someone who does not want or is unable to look after their baby in those early weeks. Or they may appeal to a mother who has a large family already and just doesn't have time to sort the baby out too. Some mothers don't like the way they take over the baby completely, but they do get them into a four-hourly routine.

Mother's help

IF YOU prefer a less hands-on approach, and need some help around the house with general work as well as children, a mother's help may fit your requirements.

A mother's help may not have any formal qualifications, but would work a full day, and could well be living in. If they come from overseas they would probably want to study English in the evenings. You can virtually specify what you want them to do to help around the house, but the emphasis is on the word 'help'. They are there to help you, rather than to replace you. That doesn't mean that you couldn't leave the children in their care at all, but it is unlikely that this kind of support would suit a mother with more than a part-time job.

AU PAIR/AU PAIR PLUS

THERE ARE regulations laid down by the Home Office about the terms and conditions of appointing an au pair. Leaflets are available from the Home Office from the address at the end of this book. Everyone has heard of the term au pair, but the detail of their role within a family is less clear. Briefly:

- An au pair is a young person, aged between 17 and 27, who comes to the UK for the purpose of learning English

- She will live with a host family and should have the opportunity to study

- She will help in the house for up to five hours a day in return for an allowance (minimum of £35 per week) and she will have two free days a week

- She can be expected to do light housework: hoovering, dusting, ironing, changing beds and so on, but not heavy housework, and she can be expected to look after children

- However, she is not qualified in childcare. She may have younger brothers and sisters at home, but she certainly couldn't be expected to take on the role of sole charge carer for babies. Because of this, she may be best suited to a family where the parents are around part of the time, or where the children have reached school age.

AN AU PAIR PLUS is the same as an au pair, but in return for working up to seven hours a day, five days a week, can expect £45–£50 in pocket money a week.

If your au pair comes from an EU country (Austria, Belgium, Denmark, Finland, France, Germany, Greece, Irish Republic, Italy, Luxembourg, Netherlands, Norway, Portugal, Spain and Sweden), then she will not need a work permit and does not have a time limit over here.

But if your au pair comes from outside the EU she will need to take a letter of invitation from her host family to her British Embassy in order to apply for a visa, which will be valid for a maximum period of two years.

Advantages of the au pair scheme

Cost effective

If you fill the bill, in that you have space in your house, and don't have any very young children, then hiring an au pair is a cheap method of combining childcare and domestic help.

Serving a mutual need

Your au pair is here to learn the language, so will be keen to become involved with you, your family and the local community. She will also be paid for what she does, which gives her pocket-money too.

Babysitting service

You can be flexible with the hours your au pair does. You may find that she is willing to trade giving a long day's work for a long weekend off to do some travelling, for example. There is no rule that says her hours have to be done during the day, so you could get babysitting done by her too. If you wanted extra babysitting, you could pay her separately for it.

Educational

The good news is an au pair will be educating your children about another culture. Just as they are learning something new, so are your children, who will learn about a different country and the way things are done abroad. If they are older, they may pick up some of the language. But the bad news is . . . that the au pair may initially have a limited vocabulary, which may make it more difficult for the children to communicate with her.

DISADVANTAGES OF THE AU PAIR SCHEME

Not trained in childcare

IT WOULD not be fair to the au pair or your children to leave her in sole charge on a regular basis. She may be very capable of looking after children, but she has no formal qualifications and probably little experience. She is not a cheap solution for regular childcare. She will not have been vetted in the way that childminders and nursery staff are.

She may not even like children

IT IS possible. She is in Britain to learn about our culture. She may well go through the motions of looking after the children, which she'll probably do very well, but she doesn't have to want to interact with them all the time.

More responsibility

SOMEONE SAID that having an au pair is a bit like looking after your friend's teenage daughter – it's another set of responsibilities. She may be only 17, and therefore need a little guidance about 'life' in general. It really depends on the au pair you appoint.

No contract

THE NATURE of the agreement is non-contractual – if she wants to go somewhere better, then she will go.

Car insurance

YOU MAY need to extend your car insurance if she is to have use of the car, and this could be expensive if she is a young, inexperienced driver.

Hilly runs an au pair and nanny agency and comments: *'If only I could have a farm to grow au pairs: they are very much in demand. An au pair is likely to want a nice family atmosphere, and no overworking. Make sure that they know the guidelines, and don't expect too much of them. Remember that they are young girls. They need telling what they can and can't do. They tend to stay for six months to a year.'*

Louise has used both nannies and au pairs, so is able to compare them: *'I think that there are different times in your life when one is more appropriate than the other. After my first child was born, I used a nursery, but when I had my second, I started to use a nanny. I was working for three days a week at this point and having someone in the house was the most convenient method of childcare for me, as well as it being cheaper for two children. Our third child, Saskia, was born and I was back at work again within three or four weeks. I must have been mad, but they needed me at work.*

But a thunderbolt struck when Saskia was diagnosed as having leukaemia when she was six months old. We spent from May to November in hospital. Our nanny was coming in three days a week, and she offered to come in for another day for free, which was really good of her but we felt that we had to pay her. Having a nanny at this stage was great – we couldn't have used an au pair; we needed someone to work longer hours than that, and who had a commitment to childcare, as the older two were obviously having to take a back seat to Saskia's illness.

Once the immediate danger was over and Saskia was at home I really had to be with her. Now I wasn't working we couldn't really afford a nanny four days a week, so reluctantly we let ours go. I started thinking about getting an au pair – mainly as another pair of hands.

Having grown so used to one particular nanny it was difficult to start all over again with a stranger – building up trust and so on. I was quite concerned at first about the question of abuse of hospitality, but it hasn't really happened. You have to be broad-minded, and give a bit of leeway, but it's easier to spot these things with itemised phone bills, for example.'

OTHER parents who have taken on au pairs share similar experiences, both good and bad:

'What I like about the au pairs we've had is that they are flexible and good with school-age children. They can babysit for a couple of evenings a week too.'

'You tend to get problems of adolescence: romance, late nights, diffidence in the morning, losing privacy.'

'If they like children it's a plus – they don't all. Try to find out if they have brothers or sisters.'

'It's good to have an extra pair of hands. I just wanted someone for two or three hours here and there, I didn't necessarily want someone around the whole day.'

'We are lucky to have enough space, but you have to make the girl feel as though it's her home and she's part of the family. You may have to compromise on your privacy, but usually it's worth it.'

'You shouldn't expect too much from them.'

'It gives you time to do things which the children don't want to do, and time to go off on your own.'

FINDING AN AU PAIR

AGAIN, LIKE nannies, a lot of agencies, both in this country and abroad, can supply au pairs.

An agency is likely (though not all do) to charge a registration fee, and a placement fee when the right person has been found for you. Sometimes there is a trial period of two to four weeks.

Jenny runs a nanny and au pair agency, and she has this advice to offer about au pairs: *'They are in demand, so it's worth looking after them. If you expect them to do too much work or babysitting, then don't be surprised if they leave after seeing a better job elsewhere. Having an au pair is great if you've got the right one.'*

ISSUES PARENTS NEED TO DISCUSS

Trust

Essential in this kind of working relationship. If you are not happy with some aspect of her behaviour, discuss it openly with her – you may have misinterpreted it.

Privacy

Try to make her privacy as important as yours, and her own room as comfortable as possible. Equally, be prepared to give up some of your privacy for the time your au pair is with you.

Emergencies

Ask your au pair if she has a basic knowledge of First Aid, if not, why not go on a day's course with her.

Sex, smoking and other vices

There's no reason why your carer shouldn't be sexually active – but what about in your house? If you don't mind, say so, and if you do, say so too. Honesty will save any embarrassing situations later on. The same would apply to anything else that you don't want to happen in your house.

Use and abuse of facilities . . .

Where is the acceptable line between taking advantage of hospitality and feeling a part of the family? It varies from person to person. It is worth thinking about what is and isn't acceptable to you and being clear and direct from the start. Then there is no danger of any misunderstanding.

CHAPTER *ten* *Informal childcare and after school options*

CHANGING NEEDS

YOUR NEEDS change as your children and family grow. There is a period in your family's life when childcare has to be absolute. When your child is very young, the carer has to be gentle but firm. With toddlers, the carer should provide constant supervision to ensure that as your children discover the world, they aren't harmed by it. Toddlers need someone guiding them in their development, and they need someone to take them to toddler groups and give them a safe haven from which they can move as they start to socialise.

From the nursery stage through their later secondary school years, they will be left with other supervising adults, but still need taking to and fro, and, if they are not to be 'latch-key kids', supervised after school.

Then there is the stage of your children not being adults, yet being quite competent on their own in many situations. They need support, but they don't need supervision. What do you do with them at this stage, which could be at around 14 or 15, depending on how mature your child is?

You may feel that, however old your child is, they still need formal childcare and prefer them to go to a childminder after school. Another option which many parents will have already discovered when looking for pre-school childcare is informal childcare: a neighbour, a friend

---

QUESTIONS TO ASK YOURSELF ABOUT YOUR CHILDREN

Are they mature? Are they responsible? Do they have a good sense of safety precautions?

Do they feel happy about being left? Are they nervous?

Where do you live? Is it close to school? Can they travel home with someone? Is there someone they can call on if they want to?

How long will they be alone? Can you organise it so it's not every night?

who also has children but does not work, or works different hours, a relation; it is worth exploring all avenues. These arrangements have the advantages of being flexible, cheap (often no money changes hands, just reciprocal favours) and reliable.

Neighbours

SALLY CHOSE to use a network of neighbours: *'I live in a small mews-type development. There are neighbours at home, and they know that the children are around, and can call on them. It may not be ideal but it's only for an hour or so.'*

NEIGHBOURS CAN be an enormous source of support. How well do you know yours? Many parents find that spending time at home after their baby is born is the first time they have got to know neighbours. This is where groups like the National Childbirth Trust are so useful, because they help to introduce people to each other. It is sometimes hard to make that first move of talking to someone you don't know, but can often pay off in terms of new friends with similar experiences to your own.

Laura's little girl has now started school, but she goes home with her neighbour's children and waits there for just over an hour for Laura's return. *'I pay her for doing this for me – and she has a nanny who does the run anyway, but you have to stay in credit. If you can't return the favour, then you must pay up.'*

Friends and acquaintances

IT'S NOT just those in the immediate vicinity that can help with childcare, but others you may have got to know through toddler group, ante-natal groups and so on.

Carolyn was going back to work earlier than she had planned, and felt that this in itself was a big enough disruption to her family, without introducing them to a stranger: *'My husband's job was flexible, so at first we could juggle pick-ups. My son, Tom, was going through a transition time: he was just starting at playgroup and I didn't want him to have to cope with other changes, so Mike managed to pick him up. Chloe, who had already* started nursery, was picked up by Anna, who she already knew from the playgroup.

Although Anna wasn't qualified, I felt safer with someone I knew. I felt very wary about leaving them with someone I hadn't known for very long. It also meant it was less of an adjustment for the children to make.

In fact, Tom has settled in very well at play-group, so on the days I work, Anna takes him home with her and then picks up Chloe after school. It helps that she's got plenty of Thomas the Tank Engine tapes for Tom to watch, as we don't have a television at home, and Tom is mesmerised.'

PARENTAL RESPONSIBILITY

It is important to remember that it is the parents who are responsible for their children until they are 16, and although others may care for them, it is parents who must take ultimate responsibility for their well being.

Eleanor solved her own childcare problems by sharing childcare with the friend who did the same job of air stewardess. *'When I had my first baby, I didn't intend going back to work, the options available were very much full time or nothing. I took my maternity leave of seven months and kept my options open. I'm glad I did because things were beginning to change, and cabin crew had more choices opening up.*

I went for an option that meant I worked roughly no more than half a working month. The nature of the job meant that I would need irregular childcare, and my family all live up in Scotland. But I had a friend who was in the same business, who didn't have any family support either, so we decided to have each other's children for a fortnight each.

One good thing about the arrangement was that the children grew up like brother and sister. They got very close, they each gained a companion and learned how to socialise, and they were still with familiar people.

Another advantage of it was that it didn't cost anything, and that has to be a major factor when it comes to childcare.

But there were things that weren't so good. We both felt that we didn't have enough time on our own with our children as we were either working for a fort-night, or we were looking after the two of them. There was nothing in between. Added to that, it could only work when we had two children in total. I've now got another little one, and my friend is pregnant. Neither of us could cope with four children, even if it was practical. Think about trying to go shop-ping with four – on second thoughts, don't. You wouldn't be able to take them anywhere, so although it was good for a while, and certainly saw both of us through that early stage of parenthood, it couldn't last for ever.'

Relatives

THIS IS another rich source of support, although the day-to-day support that families used to be able to give each other is now less practical with the growing mobility of the population. There are many advantages of keeping childcare within the family:

● Cost
Childcare is expensive and many people simply cannot afford childminders, nannies or nurseries. If you are lucky enough to have access to good, free childcare, then use it.

● A pleasure, not a burden

Many grandparents are very keen to get more involved with their growing family – particularly if they have retired or one of them is left on their own. They may be pleased to be asked and know that they are helping out. However, it is worth remembering that

---

THE CHILDREN ACT 1989

It is illegal to pay for someone to care for a child under eight outside that child's home for more than two hours a day, unless the carer is a relative, or unless the carer is registered by the local authority.

---

they are not as young as they used to be, and small children can be very tiring – don't let pleasure become a burden.

● Familiar to children

There is no adjusting to new faces and personalities. These are people whom the children have known all their lives, almost as familiar as you are, if they live close by.

● Children communicate with 'older people'

It always seems a bit of a shame that we tend to mix with our own age group and no other. It starts from preschool groups, and seems to go on from there. Teenagers mix with teenagers, young single people mix with other young, single people, and the elderly mix with other elderly people. Whilst there's a lot to be said for having friends in the same peer group we can often gain a broader range of experience and knowledge from mixing across the age groups. The benefits to both child and grandparent are clear: both can learn and gain from the other.

● Can still leave them if sick

If your child was very ill, then naturally it's likely you would want to look after them yourself, but in most cases, your relatives are glad to help out, whereas a childminder or nursery may ask you to keep your child at home until any infection has cleared up.

● They know what your standards are

The nice thing about families is that so much is already known. Your family will know what you expect, how you behave towards the children, what they should be doing. If they aren't allowed sweets during the day, then you have someone who already knows that. Sometimes life isn't so simple: they may know how you do it, but decide to do it their way, which could cause a rift. Or do you try to turn a blind eye because of all the advantages in the arrangement and you don't want to upset your family?

Lydia is now back at work, and her son Oliver is being looked after by her mother, who lives close by. *'My mother offered to look after Oliver when I went back to work, as well as her other grandson, William. She is disabled, but she said it would keep her going. It made it so much easier for me that I was leaving him with mum, because I found it very hard to go back to work anyway, and this eased the process. It helped that he'd spent time at his grandma's and knew her well. He and William get on really well together, although William is more outgoing, Oliver has learnt to hold his own.*

It's very good having a family close by, but of course there is a down side. For example, if you are paying someone, you can say what you want, but it's more difficult for me to do that. She won't take any money, but she's bought a double buggy, highchairs, nappies, you name it. It makes it difficult to be critical, because it sounds ungrateful, which I'm not. But I have to be diplomatic about some things. Oliver has a coat that I really like, but that mum can't stand, so she always puts him in something else. That makes me all the more determined that he wears it.

Having said that, I think she's diplomatic too — she knows when to back off, and she keeps quiet at the right moment.

We have always been very supportive to each other as a family and now we all babysit for each other and have Sunday lunch as a family. It's bedlam, because of all the children, but it's also good fun.'

Are there any disadvantages?

BEFORE YOU ask your parents to give childcare, it may be worth having a long, hard think. Is there anything that was difficult for you in your childhood? What if this cropped up again when they are looking after your children? Do you find it easy to be direct with your parents, or do they have a certain amount of control over you still? How would you react if they did something you didn't agree with? Would you be able to talk it over rationally, or would you both revert to a parent/child relationship?

Even if you don't use informal childcare as your main caring solution, it could come in very useful when you need childcare at short notice. If your childminder rings up to say that her daughter has chicken-pox and she can't take your child for a fortnight, you will need someone to fill in the gap.

SCHOOL DAYS

IF YOU are at the stage where your child just needs care after school then you could still ask a friend, neighbour or relative to help out, or you could investigate after-school childminders, after-school play schemes and Kids' Clubs. With an increasing number of women returning to work, more single parent families, an increase in juvenile crime, after-school and school holiday care will become a major issue for parents and government alike.

After–school childminder

IF YOU are already using a childminder, you may well find that she is willing to continue looking after your child, picking up and dropping off. This can be very useful if they start part time. But if you want her to do this, you should think about where you want your child to go to school, and how convenient that will be for the childminder. Does she have transport? Does she have children that need picking up from another school at the same time?

It may be difficult to find a true after-school childminder in your area who prefers to just have children after school, when their children are at home anyway. It's worth making enquiries at your local Social Services office to get a list of registered minders.

Often such childminders are best found by word of mouth; ask other parents what they do, or ask your own children what their friends do.

After-school play schemes

THESE ARE beginning to blossom. There are different types: some schemes are run by schools, from, say, 3.30pm until 5.30 or 6pm. Local councils also run them, on a free-of-charge first-come, first-served basis. You may want to know if there are any schools in your area that run them before you choose which school to apply for.

John is a Play Manager for his local council. *'We have six play-centres, which are open access, meaning that children come and go between opening hours, rather than be dropped off and picked up at pre-arranged times. They are open 52 weeks a year; in term times, from 5pm until 9pm, and in the holidays from 11am until 4pm, and 5pm until 8pm (the staff take a break at 4pm and most children go home for their tea). They are aimed at all children between the ages of five and 16.*

There is also an after-school club, which has a bus to pick children up from local schools and take them to one school until the parents' pick-up time. During the summer holidays, there are fun schemes running. Some cost about £1.25 a day and last from 11am until 3pm. There is also a day-care scheme which is more expensive at about £47 a week, but this is from 8.30am until 5.30pm, for five- to 12-year-olds. Contact your local council to find out what schemes they can offer in your area.'

Private after-school schemes

THEY ARE often run in a building attached to a primary school. When school finishes, the staff meet the children who are staying on in the school hall. They have tea, and then play games like tag. It provides a safe environment, enjoyment, and a chance to play with friends until picked up by parents.

Private schools

SOME PRIVATE schools have 'prep' time after school, which means that the children can stay behind and be supervised while they do their homework. This gives the parents some extra time before picking them up, and means the homework is out of the way.

Kids' Club Network (KCN)

THERE IS growing evidence that the number of Kids' Clubs will treble over the next two years. However, there may still be a serious shortage of after-school care provision. KCN believes that an after-school club is needed near or at every school – some 25,000 clubs to meet demand.[1]

In a recent British Social Attitudes Survey, 25% of children under 12 whose mothers worked full-time said that they look after themselves after school and during school holidays.[2]

KIDS' CLUB NETWORK

Kids' Club Network (see Directory for contact information) is a charity which offers:

- Help and support to those starting up a Kids' Club
- Advice and information to government and local authorities about after-school care
- Helpline for parents and playworkers
- Training for playcare workers
- A number of publications
- Fund-raising advice
- Consultancy service for employers on childcare support for their employees.

THE SCHOOL HOLIDAYS

SO YOU'VE got your children organised during term time, but then the school holidays arrive – you may have to think again. According to Kids' Club Network, the difference between office and school hours is 750 hours, most of which take place over holidays.

[1, 2 Report of the All Parliamentary Group on Parenting and International Year of the Family UK. Parliamentary Hearings, 1994.]

Perhaps this is the time when grandparents who live a long way away could help – why not send your children to stay with them for a fortnight? The children would probably love it – an adventure away from home, but with the security of grandparents. And of course it would give you a break – a chance to recharge those batteries and go out without having to organise a babysitter three weeks in advance.

Annual holidays

SOME PARENTS find this one of the hardest things to accept – no longer can you have your holiday out of school time, when the prices are halved and the beaches are empty. Other parents are happy to take their children out of school for a couple of weeks, which may be cheaper and more relaxing, but doesn't help solve the search for childcare during the school holidays.

School friends

AS THE children grow up, so they make new school friends. Maybe you can have an arrangement where parents take turns to occupy a small group of friends for a day or two.

Local schemes

AGAIN, YOUR local council may run schemes throughout the holidays in local schools. They may be run privately, or by the council, but a lot of them are very reasonably priced and the children seem to thoroughly enjoy them. Sometimes they don't start till 9.30 or 10am, and finish at 3.30pm, but you could arrange alternate weeks with your partner or a friend to fetch and carry.

Private schemes

MORE AND more companies are realising that there is a very obvious need, particularly during school holidays, for employees' children to be cared for safely whilst their parents are working.

The idea is based on the summer camps in the USA. One scheme started in 1989, catering for the children of single parent families in the local borough. The aim was to offer children the chance to experiment with different sports and activities. That particular scheme is going from strength to strength. The founders were recently awarded the tender for the play scheme of a large British company and have continued from there.

Jane works for a company who will be running a play scheme during the summer holidays. *'This is the third year that the scheme has been running. We expanded to 75 children last year, and this year there is room for 100, because it is so popular. Because this is a big company, there is the space and the demand to run our own scheme, but I know smaller companies often pool together and buy in a number of places for their employees.*

This scheme is offered to the children of all the employees, whether male or female, full or part time. The children range from five-year-olds, if they are starting nursery care, up to about 13 or 14. What this does is take away the worry of childcare for a few weeks. It is subsidised by the company, and children can opt in for one week or six weeks, or the same days over that period. There is a range of activities, and a couple of outings each week.

As employers are looking for workers, they need to be able to offer something to working parents. I think this is a good thing to offer as part of an employment package.'

David runs a play scheme: *'We will either get a tender to work with one company, or we can hire out a school or another safe building, and smaller companies can buy a number of places.*

There's no fixed time for the children to arrive — anywhere between 8 and 10am and for that period there is what we call free play, where they can choose what they want to do, from a number of activities like: video corner, dressing-up, computers, table tennis, snooker, ball games and team games like unihoc.

Then during the day other activities become available: archery, aerobics, badminton, basketball, face painting, video filming.

We have between 24 and 100 children, depending on the camp. They stay in the same group all week, and each week has a different theme running through it. Our ratio of carer to children is 1:8 maximum.

We try to make sure that everyone gets a chance to do everything that they want to, and our staff are generally people who are involved in child-related courses and have previous experience of working with children. This isn't just a summer job.'

THESE SCHEMES are on the increase and there are both day and residential camps throughout the country.

Probably the most well known of these is Camp Beaumont, which has a selection of camps, both day camps and residential. Each camp incorporates a nursery camp, where the younger children are looked after and their different needs met. The list of activities is endless, from Duplo and Playdoh for the little ones, to go-karting, judo, squash, water polo, fencing and fashion design for the older ones. There's also riding, golf and tennis for those in their teenage years.

Although these options aren't cheap, it does give your children a great deal of stimulation in an active but safe environment.

The Children Act stipulates that these schemes must be regulated and the British Activity Holiday Association invites schemes to become members and submit to annual inspections to check adherence to safety standards.

If you think your colleagues could benefit from such a scheme, why not suggest it to your managing director, who may realise it would be of equal benefit to the company.

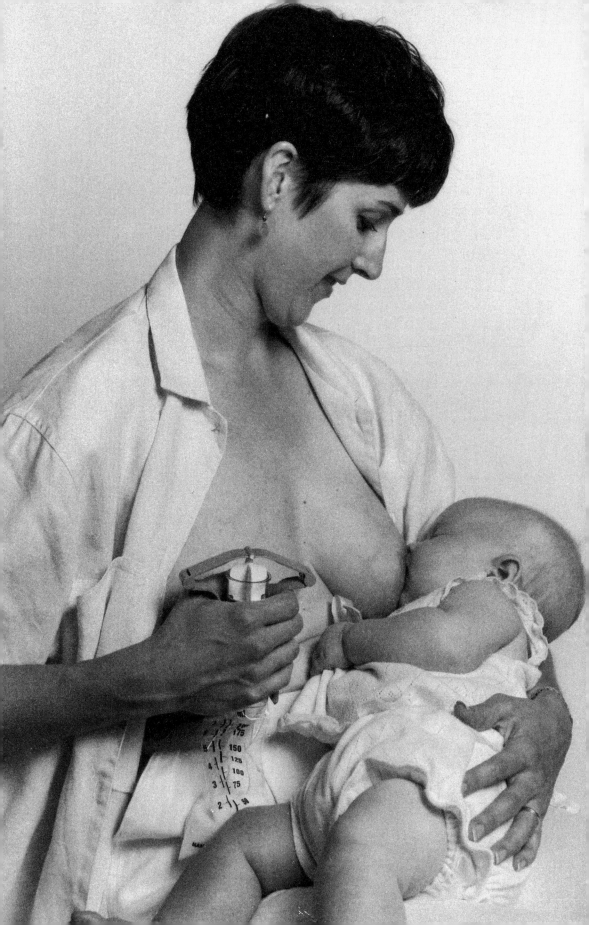

CHAPTER *eleven*

Breastfeeding and working

ONE OF THE issues of returning to work is when or whether to wean your baby off the breast. Of course, many people will already have stopped breastfeeding, but if you haven't, and are considering the angles you can look at this from, then this chapter is for you.

As with all things child-related, the best solution is likely to be based on individual circumstances, personal preferences, and what makes your family the least stressed. Yet again there are no right or wrong answers, just what is right or wrong for you. The transition from 100% nurturing to spreading oneself across a number of roles can be turbulent. Spending time thinking about how to make the journey as smooth as possible is likely to pay off very quickly.

A decision about continuing to breastfeed when returning to work is probably going to hinge on some of the following factors:

- The age of your baby
- The method of feeding up till now
- The work style you will be adopting
- The preference of your baby
- Your feelings.

YOUR FEELINGS could be the most important factor in the equation. Some mothers like to have a 'clean break' from the role of nursing mother and primary carer – not because they suddenly go off their child, but because they find the quality of the roles incompatible, and prefer to settle into the new regime with clearly defined lines. Others prefer to maintain breastfeeding because it makes the return to work that much easier by continuing the closeness of nursing.

DO YOU HAVE TO GIVE UP?

THERE IS absolutely no reason why you should stop breastfeeding when you return to work. Your body can adjust to any changes in supply, given a reasonable amount of warning (more of that later in the chapter), and although most people who do it don't find it easy all the time, or certainly as easy as when you are at home full time, they generally feel a great sense of achievement and satisfaction that they have continued giving their baby the best source of nutrition whilst being away from the baby for part of the day.

For those who work from home, this is less of a problem. The mother can simply feed during her lunch hour, or coffee break. But for those who are returning to work away from home, the idea of giving up feeding as well as adjusting to the separation can sometimes seem traumatic. It can also change the perspective on the whole process. For example, some mothers simply assume that they will give up feeding when they return to work, then find that the baby is reluctant to take a bottle. This can feed feelings of guilt into a mother who may be experiencing some guilt anyway – 'not only am I leaving my baby, but she will starve when I am away, too.'

Having a deadline to meet can put intolerable pressure upon a woman in this situation, but it is worth applying some lateral thinking to the issue – sometimes the answer is there staring at you, only you're too worried to see it. For example, it is worth asking your employer for an extra month's maternity leave. Stranger things have happened – they may say yes. Or, rather than making the separation more traumatic than it need be, you carry on breastfeeding, thus maintaining the exclusive relationship with your baby and making the separation less dramatic for both of you: although one big thing has changed in your lives, another thing is staying exactly the same.

If it is the case that a mother had decided to give up breastfeeding to prepare for the return, then found the whole process very difficult and subsequently decided to carry on feeding, the sense of relief can be enormous, and it can really have an impact on how the mother feels about going back to work, making the transition a much more positive event.

Reasons to continue breastfeeding

'Good, mumsy start to the day'

LAURA FOUND the closeness of that early morning breastfeeding session a good start: *'When you are on the go all day long, and this is whether you go out to work or not, it's good to begin with a relaxing cuddle in bed. The two of you can spend those extra few minutes in bed, without the dash downstairs to warm the bottle while the baby cries and your eyes are barely opened.'* Because the milk-producing hormone is at its most active overnight, it also means that the early morning feed is plentiful, thus giving the baby a good, nutritious start to her day.

Maintaining the bond

THIS IS something that only a baby's mother can do for her, and that can be very important too, if she is going to be left with someone else. It means that you are undoubtedly her mother, providing her with something that only you, as her mother, can deliver.

That relaxing time . . .

ONE OF the great things about breastfeeding is that you (well usually) have a sit down when you're doing it. For the working mother, this can be the opportunity to grasp at with both hands: a chance to sit and relax, and know that your baby is being satisfied at the same time. There are not many opportunities for doing this, and you are likely to be praised for sitting, with your feet up, relaxing with your baby. Make the most of it.

'I had a lot of trouble starting – I'm damned if I'm going to stop now' Kerrie

LOTS OF mothers, like Kerrie, find the going pretty tough when they start breastfeeding, but they stick it out. It can sometimes take about six weeks for the system to settle down – if you are returning to work when your baby is about three months, there is barely time to enjoy it before stopping again. This is why Kerrie wasn't going to stop, having expended so much effort on getting going. She says: *'I had lots of trouble for weeks after the birth, I was cracked and bleeding, but I persevered because I was determined to do it. Also I had a caesarean so I felt that I wanted to do the feeding right. I got depressed for the first eight weeks, which I felt was due to the feeding, but after that, it went like a dream.'* Once you do reach that stage of finding the whole thing a complete doddle, it seems such a shame to stop.

Early returners

IF YOU ARE going back to work with quite a young baby, continuing to breastfeed is reassuring because you know that the baby is still getting the best food.

BREASTFEEDING – HOW IT WORKS

How does it work?

TWO HORMONES, oxytocin and prolactin, are what makes breastfeeding work. They establish the production line of milk, one being responsible for the ejection reflex which gets the milk out of your breast and into the baby's mouth, and the other looks after the supply, getting the message from the suckling of the baby to make more milk. So it isn't just a case of the baby sucking the milk out. The baby's suckling stimulates those hormones and gets your production process working. You are working as a team to make enough milk for your baby.

Supply and demand

THE IDEA here is that the baby, if allowed to feed on demand, which means offering the breast when it is asked for, is able to make you create the right amount of milk. One question that is often asked of breastfeeding counsellors is how you know how much milk the baby is getting. When you can easily see how much the baby is taking with a bottle, it might seem that this is a very reasonable criticism of breastfeeding. But if your breasts are not sore, if your baby is producing wet and dirty nappies (it must be coming from somewhere!), if she is gaining weight and seems contented after a feed, it's very likely that your baby is getting the perfect amount for her needs. Trust yourself, you can make just the right amount, even though you can't see it.

Let down reflex

THIS IS the mother's response to the baby's suckling. Some mothers find that their breasts tingle when it starts to happen, and what is actually happening is

FACTFILE ON GOODNESS

Breast milk is a changing fluid – it adapts to the needs of the age of the baby.

'During the first year of breastfeeding the protein content of the breast milk gradually falls, regardless of the mother's diet. This is compensated for by the fact that most babies are given amounts of solid foods from about six months and these provide the extra protein necessary for growth. The fall-off in protein is paralleled by a normal reduction in growth rate.'

Breast is Best 1983: Stanway & Stanway, Pan.

Positive effect of breastfeeding against infection.

'Breastfeeding during the first 13 weeks of life confers protection against gastrointestinal illness that persists beyond the period of breastfeeding itself.'

Howie, et al: Positive Effect of Breastfeeding Against Infection, BMJ Vol. 300, 6.1.90.

Wherever there is love, there is oxytocin.

'Oxytocin is involved in foreplay and in male and female orgasm. It is also released before and during suckling the baby. Oxytocin is the hormone of altruism, the forgetting of oneself.' The practical effect of this is that breastfeeding is not only good for the baby – it is good for the mother too, as it helps her to relax and unwind. There can be a sense of a deep sigh of relief as the milk flows to the baby and the mother can sit, relax, enjoy and the pressures of life slip away.

Michel Odent 1992: The Nature of Birth and Breastfeeding. Bergin & Garvey.

that the breasts are starting to send the milk down to the areola for the baby to take. So whilst there is always milk there for the baby to feed from at the beginning of the feed, the let down sends further supplies. If you have a good supply you may well find that your other breast starts to drip when the let down happens. And the other thing about the let down is that it doesn't always happen when your baby is feeding. Sometimes it gets triggered by seeing a baby, hearing a baby crying, thinking about your baby. Again, not everybody experiences this, and very often if it happens in the first few weeks, it dies down once the supply is established.

Positioning

GETTING THE baby well positioned at the breast is a key factor in successful breastfeeding. If the baby isn't well positioned, she may:

- Hurt you. A poorly positioned baby can feel excruciating to the mother, can cause cracked or bleeding nipples, and can make every feed a miserable experience and one that is dreaded by the mother
- Reduce your milk supply. Generally, the poorly positioned baby is not taking enough of the areola, but sucking on the nipple instead. This means that she is not sending a strong enough message to your body to make more milk
- Want frequent feeding. There's no getting away from it, many breastfed babies feed more frequently than their bottle-fed counterparts. But the baby who is in need of new positioning may not be getting adequate access to the breast milk because her mouth isn't open wide enough. This means that she will be hungry sooner than she need be.

BUT IF you are experiencing problems with your feeding, you may like to contact an NCT breastfeeding counsellor, who can talk about your individual needs. You don't have to be a member of the NCT in order to talk to a counsellor, there is no charge for the service, and you don't have to be committed to breastfeeding for the next two years. All counsellors will support mothers who want to stop feeding and don't know how to go about it. (See addresses in Directory.)

NIGHT-TIME WITH YOUR BABY

UNLESS YOU are working from home, and even then to a certain extent, you are likely to see less of your baby. There can be two spin-offs from this. The first is that you miss your baby, and that can make you feel sad, or guilty, or just that you want to spend as much time as possible with her when you're at home. The second is that you may be breastfeeding her less, or using a pump to express at work. This can have the effect of reducing the milk supply. Plenty of feeding when you are at home can help to overcome this, and keep you close to your baby.

If your baby still wakes for feeds overnight, you may prefer her to sleep in the same room as you. It is important that your baby does not get overheated, and the Foundation for the Study of Infant Deaths recommends that babies sleep in a cot next to the parent's bed for at least the first six months. Even so, you can bring your baby into bed to

POSITIONING

Signs of a well-positioned baby

- Wide-open mouth
- Tongue underneath breast
- Bottom lip turned out
- Cheeks not drawn in
- Movement around temple or ears
- Mother not sore
- Baby's lower jaw taking good mouthful of areola
- Periods of fast and slow feeding

The other thing to remember about breastfeeding is that, as long as the baby is in a straight line, so that her neck or her body doesn't have to turn in order to reach the breast, you can feed her in any position.

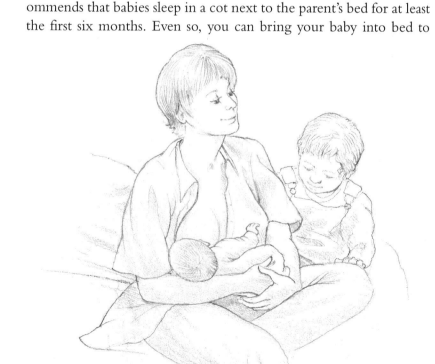

feed without having to get up, and you can rest whilst breastfeeding her. Although nighttime feeding can be very tiring, particularly if you have to work the next day, it is reassuring to know that these night feeds will be helping to maintain your milk supply.

However, some parents still prefer to sleep with their babies in the same bed. It means that you can feed your baby and sleep at the same time, thus keeping up your milk supply and resting too. Some babies are more settled if they are in bed with their parents, rather than alone in a cot. It means that if the baby awakes, the breast is no more than a turn away, rather than you having to fetch the baby and settle her afterwards. And it means that you are spending more time together.

EXPRESSING MILK

THE ADVANTAGE of this system is that you can give your baby breast milk, even when you are at work and you know that your baby is still receiving optimum nutrition when you are away. Expressing your milk means that other people can feed the baby, from a bottle, or from a beaker.

Expressing milk is removing milk from the breast, without the assistance of a baby. There are a number of ways of doing this:

- Expressing by hand
- Expressing by hand-held pump
- Expressing by battery/mains-aided pump
- Expressing by electric pump.

Distasteful?

SOME PEOPLE just don't like the idea of expressing. It makes them feel cow-like, or they feel uncomfortable handling their own breasts. There is also a distinction to be drawn between the types of pump. Some women prefer to hand express because they feel that being attached to a pump is, somehow, not quite right. Others find the machines by far the most effective way of pumping.

Finally, before going into more detail about expressing, it's worth remembering that, generally speaking, pumping takes time. We all know somebody who can express eight ounces at the drop of a hat, but for most of us, this is another skill to be learnt, that takes patience, sometimes privacy, and, of course, no item about breastfeeding would be complete without a mention of . . . perseverance. So, if you want to make a go of it, keep at it.

What if you don't want to express?

EVERYONE IS told that breastfeeding is best for the baby, and it gets easier and so on. But what if you don't want to? Some mothers feel under pressure to breastfeed: maybe their partner feels strongly, maybe their peer group are all breastfeeding.

Sometimes adjusting to the return to work is quite enough to deal with, without the added pressure of 'Should I, shouldn't I pump'. For mothers who feel like this, it may be that everybody will be happier if they do exactly what is right for them and their family.

Laura didn't express milk, but carried on feeding night and morning. *'I didn't express because my baby was six months old by the time I went back to work so I didn't think I needed to. She was old enough to take other nourishment as well.'*

Your flexible friend

IF YOU DO like the idea of continuing to breastfeed, one of the great advantages is its flexibility. You can feed as much or as little as you want. For example, you can just feed mornings and evenings, which removes any need to express, or you can ensure that your baby is completely breastfed, by expressing during the day when you are at work.

Very often babies like to be fed in the evenings. If you opt for feeding mornings and evenings only, the long evening feed can mean that you're spending more time with your baby, and also you're helping to keep up your milk supply.

The principle of supply and demand comes into its own here. The more your baby feeds, the more milk you make. Likewise, the less your baby feeds, the less milk you make. So if you intend to feed twice daily only, your body will adapt to that regime, and you should be able to supply your baby with her needs.

Guidelines for expressing

- When you express milk, you will make more milk. If you are building up a supply in advance of returning to work, it is worth looking out for signs of engorgement
- If you are planning to feed just mornings and evenings, give your body time to adjust to the new regime. Drop feeds slowly, say one every second day, so that you don't experience any discomfort. If you do feel full in the middle of the day, you could express enough to make you feel comfortable
- Try to make adjustments only once your milk supply has become established, which is generally four to six weeks after birth
- Try to make any adjustments well before you return to work, so that you're not sitting at a desk with rock hard breasts, aching to release the milk
- Your hormones may not respond as well to a pump as to the baby suckling, which could mean that your supply begins to diminish. You can counteract this by offering extra feeds to the baby, say over the weekend, or extend the evening feeds
- It's worth thinking about the sort of method you want to use well in advance. The pumps aren't cheap, so it's hard to keep buying different ones on a trial and error basis. But maybe you know people whose pump you could borrow? Or otherwise it may be worth starting with the cheapest method and working up from there
- There is a risk that the baby will get to prefer the bottle. This does happen sometimes, and it may be worth thinking about how you would feel if your baby chose the time of her weaning.

Pumps and things

THERE ARE two ways of breastfeeding. One requires no more than a lactating mother and her baby. The other one is far more high-tech, and can involve electric pumps costing hundreds of pounds, travel bags, storage bags, sterilisers, bottles . . . the list is endless. At least we now have the choice to make breastfeeding what we want it to be, and if that is long-distance breastfeeding while we are at work, we now have the technology.

The cheapest method of expressing milk is by hand. Even so, you will need equipment to store it in, to collect it in, maybe to freeze it in. Hand expression works by massaging the breast with the hand and can be very effective for some. It's also worth knowing how to do it in order to relieve engorgement if it ever happens to you.

As you move up the ladder of sophistication of these pumps, so the price and the technology increases, but not necessarily the rate of success. There are hand pumps which require two hands, hand pumps which you can use with one hand, battery pumps, battery and mains pumps, electric pumps that convert to hand pumps and supersonic electric pumps that are generally available in hospitals or are hired out for short-term use.

Some mothers like to build up a good supply to keep in the freezer before they go back. This removes the pressure upon them to express every day for the next day, because on some days it may be impossible to find the time. A mother could, therefore, express after a feed once a day, for maybe a month before returning to work. Or she could express after one feed for a fortnight, and two feeds for the next fortnight. It partly depends on how much opportunity there will be to express once back in the office. If once a day is the maximum then it is probably best to leave it at that, or else your body will have to adjust to the decrease in demand when you work.

It's worth stressing that you shouldn't be discouraged by the amount of milk you make at first. There are tricks that may help, which will be mentioned later on in this chapter, but a lot of the mystery of expressing is to do with relaxing, and believing that you can do it.

Choosing your method

THIS IS a question of personal preference, which hopefully the next few pages will help you to decide upon. You could spend hundreds of pounds finding one that suits you, and buying up all the accessories, 'that every working mother can't do without', or so the manufacturers would tell you.

Many people will find that they can express by all methods, others find that only one suits them, but there are ways and means of getting the best out of your expressing experience and giving your body the greatest opportunity to get the milk flowing.

Making expressing work

RELAX IS the key word. Easier said than done? Maybe so, but once it starts, it will get easier all the time.

Some people find being in private helps them to relax completely, but others prefer someone to talk to.

Perhaps reminding yourself of those relaxation exercises for labour will help you to unwind too. Finding somewhere that is physically comfortable is important. If you are perched over a sink, or sitting on the edge of a chair it is not going to enhance your sense of calmness. An exercise of clenching muscles and slowly untensing them may make you feel more consciously relaxed.

Louise had to express in oppressive circumstances: '*I found the experience of breastfeeding at work nerve-racking. Although I had my own consulting room, I used to sit against the door and things like that. I used to say to myself, "I need this milk", and nothing would come out . . . or the pump would squeak.*'

ON THE other hand, Lucy runs workshops, and would express in the classrooms during her lunch-time without any problems.

Warmth

BEING WARM helps breast milk to flow. You could try showering and just letting the water flow over you for ten minutes or so before expressing, or you could lie in the bath. The knock-on effect of this is that it will probably relax you at the same time. Lots of people find that just soaking in a bath will start to make the milk flow as they lie there: this can be reassuring.

If you don't want to take a bath, then using warm flannels or wrapping up a hot-water bottle and laying that on your chest will have a similar effect.

The power of positive thinking

THE LET down reflex, which you need to get working if you are to express, responds to the stimulus of the baby suckling, but can also be triggered by thinking about the baby, hearing the baby. This can sometimes work against you, for example if you suddenly hear a baby crying (it doesn't even have to be yours), or someone at the office asks you about your baby, and all of a sudden, there are two damp patches on your shirt, or you feel that tingling sensation in your breasts. If this does happen to you, crossing your arms will help to stop the flow, or pushing your hand against your breast. Of course, this can look rather strange, as you sit in a committee meeting, arms tightly crossed. But don't worry, it passes in a few seconds.

Harriet used a visual aid for her pumping sessions: '*I didn't find it easy to express, but I took a photo of Ella with me to work and that seemed to do the trick.*'

SOMETIMES JUST thinking about the baby is enough to trigger the let down, or you could, like Harriet, take something that belongs to the baby with you, maybe an article of clothing or a tape of her gurgling.

Hand expressing

YOU WILL need something to express the milk into. It is easiest if the container is wide-rimmed. It will need to be sterile, and any other receptacles will also need to be sterile.

Wash your hands before starting to express.

It is easy to damage the delicate tissue of the breast, so be sure you don't push too hard.

When you start to express, don't expect to be able to do it quickly. It's worth anticipating that it will take up to 45 minutes, but the length of time will be reduced with practice.

The morning feed

ONE OF THE BEST times to express is after an early morning feed. Your body has been resting overnight, which is when it is best at making milk. Very often your supply is more abundant than your baby might need.

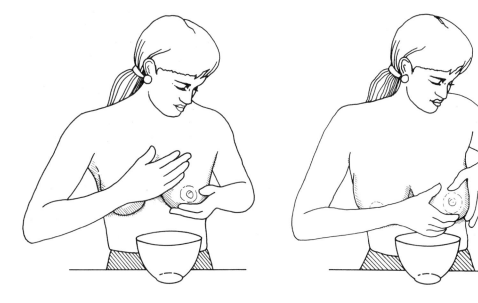

FEEDING FILE

EXPRESSING MILK BY HAND

Advantages

- No special equipment is needed, only a wide-necked sterile container and clean hands.

- Hand expressing mimics a baby's suckling action more closely than expressing by pump, so it may be a better way to maintain the milk supply.

- Expressing by hand may be gentler than expressing with a pump.

Disadvantages

- It may take longer to express by hand than by pump.

- Your hands may get tired.

How to hand express

- Use a hand to cup your breast from underneath, with your fore-finger along the line where your areola (the dark area surrounding your nipple) and breast meet. Place your thumb on top of your breast, along the same line.

- Your milk is stored in reservoirs situated approximately below this line. These reservoirs need to be squeezed gently to extract the milk. You may need to move your hand slightly in towards your nipple or back towards your chest to find the milk reservoirs – experiment until you find the right place for you.

- Gently squeeze your thumb and fingers together, pushing back and in towards your ribcage at the same time. This combined movement helps push the milk along the ducts towards the nipple, as well as squeezing it out.

- Relax the pressure, then repeat the movement.

- Your milk may take a minute or two to flow, so don't give up if nothing happens immediately.

- Move your hand around your breast, so that you cover all the milk ducts. You could also change hands on the same breast.

- If your hand gets tired, change sides, then come back to the first side later.

- Sometimes it is easier to get the knack of hand expressing after you have been shown how. Your midwife, health visitor or breastfeeding counsellor should be able to help you.

- The very best way to learn may be to watch someone who is able to do it – ask your breastfeeding counsellor if she knows someone who might show you how.

Another way of building up a store of milk is to wait for an hour or so after an early feed, when your supplies have built up again, and express as much as you can to store; then your milk will build up again for the next feed.

Of course, if you are doing this sort of thing, there may be times when your baby will be hungry earlier than you anticipate, and will be surprised when the usual amount of milk isn't there, or maybe will go longer between feeds, leaving you full and desperate to get rid of the milk. Once you get into a routine, you should find that these problems are reduced or disappear.

If you opt for expressing straight after one of your baby's feeds, your baby will have stimulated the let down reflex, so you won't be starting from cold, and another way to get the baby to help you is to use a one-hand pump, so that you can feed the baby from one breast, whilst expressing from the other. This may take some practice before it works well.

Another thing about the let down is that it doesn't only appear at the very beginning of the feed, but kicks in spasmodically during the feed. If you happen to be expressing and feel that you have run out, you may find that if you keep going a little longer, there will be another surge of milk. It is important, though, to stop expressing if you start to get sore.

Hand pumps

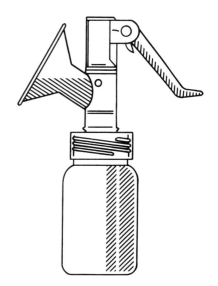

AGAIN, EVERYTHING needs to be sterile and modern pumps are easy to dismantle in order to sterilise.

This is the cheapest type of pump. Presently they cost between £10 and £16. The advantages of them are that they are relatively cheap, easily portable and quiet.

When Sarah went back to work she was happy with her hand pump: *'I used it at work twice a day, for about 15–20 minutes at a time. I was lucky because I was working in a hospital and could find places to slip into where I could express in peace. I used two sterilised bottles, which I'd put in the fridge, and it was still cold when I got home, so there were no issues about transporting.'*

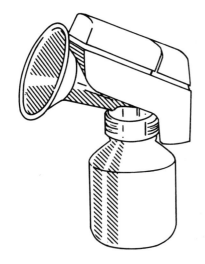

Battery pumps

THESE PUMPS are more expensive, around £25, and there are some that can convert to a mains supply too, which are around £35. The advantage of them is that it saves your hand getting worn out pumping away, though of course they will be using lots of batteries unless you get rechargeable ones. Another disadvantage is that they can be noisy, or at least, noisier than a hand pump. Sometimes this is irrelevant, but if you are reduced to expressing in the loo, you may not want the raised eyebrows of your colleagues wondering what on earth you are up to on the other side of the door.

Electric pumps

THESE ARE industrial-sized pumps. They are very heavy, cost about £400, and are generally found in Special Care Baby Units, or available for hire through organisations such as the National Childbirth Trust and La Leche League. The newer models are now coming out in more pastelly, creamy shades whereas until recently the standard issue was gunmetal grey and, it has to be said, was not an appealing sight.

Having said that, they are probably the most universally successful type of pump. Apart from their success rate, they are good because you can do dual pumping with them, which means expressing from both breasts at the same time, thus saving you time. The down side is that they are not portable and they cost about £1 a day to hire, which builds up over a period of time.

They are mainly intended for mothers of babies in special care who need to establish their milk supply without the help of the baby, and for mothers whose babies cannot feed for any other reason. They would be useful to hire for a short period to build up a supply of milk before returning to work.

Vanessa is a Pump Agent for Egnell Ameda. That means that she is involved in a branch of the NCT, and hires out pumps to those who

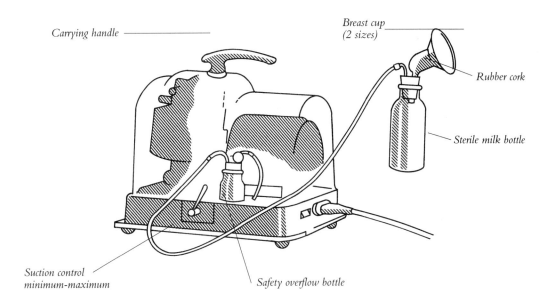

Carrying handle ——————

Breast cup
(2 sizes)

Rubber cork

Sterile milk bottle

Suction control
minimum-maximum

Safety overflow bottle

want them. She has about half a dozen of them and they are available to anyone who needs them. *'I would say that the majority of women who hire pumps are using them to establish breastfeeding, maybe if their baby has been in special care and they are now home, or they need to build up their supply. There are a number of mothers who use them to build up a store of milk before returning to work, and some hire them because for some reason their baby is refusing the breast and they want to maintain their supply.'*

THERE IS also now a small version of the electric breast pump, which is basically a hand pump with a motor attached; its advantage is that it converts to a hand pump when the need arises. That type costs about £60–£70.

Freezing

IF YOU are expressing a number of feeds during a day, you can add to the same container, but it is a good idea to cool the newly-expressed milk first for half an hour in the fridge, then add it to milk already collected. At the end of the day, the milk can be dated and frozen.

You can also add fresh milk to frozen milk, so long as there is no more than 50% fresh milk compared to frozen. In other words, if you

STORAGE

As with everything that milk is expressed into, so all storage containers must be sterile. Fresh milk can be stored in the fridge for 24 hours. If it has gone off, it won't smell right. Make sure that all milk is dated.

Storage containers:
● Plastic bottles
● Milk freezer bags. You can attach them to some pumps and express directly into them. Some of them are laminated, with a layer between the milk and the plastic
● Ice-cube trays. Not only useful for those first solids foods, but also for freezing breast milk in.

have 100ml in the freezer, you should not add more than 50ml. Milk can be frozen for up to three months in a domestic freezer, and for seven days in the freezer compartment of a fridge. If you have added fresh milk to frozen milk, the whole lot should be used by the date of the first milk.

Defrosting

ONE OF the best ways to thaw breast milk is to hold the container under cold running water and gradually add warmer water until the milk is thawed and heated to room temperature.

Breast milk should not be heated in a microwave oven, as valuable components of the milk will be destroyed if it is overheated. As microwave ovens heat liquids unevenly, hot spots in the milk may burn the baby.

BABIES AND BOTTLES

THIS IS an important section, and one that many people may be looking for in desperation, for, try as we might, there are some babies who don't like to take the bottle. Breastfeeding requires a certain way of sucking, and bottle-feeding requires another. If a baby starts to learn how to get milk effectively from a bottle, she is as likely to want to carry on sucking that way as the other way. On the other hand, some babies take to a bottle when offered one at three months and move back to the breast for the next feed.

The facts seem to be that babies get the hang of breastfeeding, and that is their perception of how to get their milk. If they have nothing to contradict that perception until they get to, say, three months, they may find it difficult to adjust to a totally different type of feeding.

Does that mean that it isn't worth starting to breastfeed if you plan to return to work?

TRANSPORTING

If you are planning on expressing at work, the milk has to get from your office to your baby, often with a waiting period in between.

There are variable factors when you decide what you need for this:

Distance

If you have an hour's journey to and from your office, then you will need something robust whereas a carrier bag with a cool pack in it would suffice for a five-minute walk.

Time of year

Although less relevant in the UK than overseas, we do get hot days here, and like any other perishable food, breast milk will go off more quickly in the heat, and will therefore need more attention paid to it in the summer.

Method of transport

Slinging a bottle of breast milk onto the back seat of your car will not elicit the same response as doing the same on the 5.38 from Waterloo, particularly if it has a sign on it saying, 'Rosie's breast milk – DO NOT DRINK' for the benefit of your work colleagues whilst it is in the fridge. Some people are sensitive to breast milk being anywhere else but in you or the baby (some people don't even

like that), and although it wouldn't be unreasonable to decide that it's their problem, they may make you feel uncomfortable.

Office conditions

Maybe your office is well-equipped, so that you can easily store your expressed breast milk (EBM) in a nearby fridge. But many offices don't have good facilities – it may not even have a fridge or if it does have, it may be down three miles of corridor and not worth the journey. Again, it is a consideration. This means that either you accept the trek to the fridge twice a day, or make sure that your own system of cool bags is second to none.

Breast milk needs to be kept chilled, in order to reduce the risk of bacteria growing. There are now travel bags specifically made for working mothers who express at work, but obviously you don't need to get one of these unless you want to. Lots of people have their own methods of transport, like Harriet: *'I expressed at work, but I didn't want anyone to know what I was doing – it's not a mother-friendly office – so I did it in the loo. I used to store it in Häagen-Dazs containers and put it in the fridge. No one ever found out . . . as far as I know.'*

On the contrary, there are still plenty of reasons to breastfeed if you are working. But there's no doubt that for some, this period of 'will she, won't she take the bottle' can be worrying and distressing.

When to start to offer the bottle

IF YOU want your baby to take a bottle, whether because you're returning to work, or so that you can have an evening out occasionally, it is a good idea to offer a bottle early in the baby's life. It is generally thought that it's best to wait until feeding is established before offering a bottle, so that the baby has a good idea of breastfeeding first, but some mothers prefer to offer the bottle earlier than that.

Amy, with four children, says: *'I didn't have any problems with my babies taking the bottle. I introduced one a week, with water in, very early, in the first couple of weeks.'*

Louise: *'I learnt the trick of giving a bottle of expressed breast milk in the first week or so to my first baby. It worked and I did it with the others, who didn't have a problem either.'*

WHICHEVER WAY you try it, there is always an element of risk that the baby will come to prefer the bottle to the breast. Sometimes it is because milk comes out more quickly from a bottle, none of this waiting around for the let down. Another reason is that as babies get

older, they start to prefer the better view they get whilst bottle-feeding. Rather than being snuggled into their mother's bosom, they are able to look upon the outside world.

Sue found that her daughter's interest moved on. *'It was cuddly, nice for her and nice for me, obviously the best thing for her, but in the end she got used to the bottle and getting the milk more quickly.'*

Getting your baby to try the bottle

THERE ARE no certain solutions. Patience, persistence, and time are all factors in this. Remember too, that your baby is not being naughty if she isn't interested in a bottle at first. She has no idea what she is being offered. Imagine what it might feel like if someone tried to push a tube of toothpaste in your mouth. Try to let her become interested in the teat, rather than forcing it into her mouth. The following is a list of mothers' suggestions:

- Her mother is the person least likely to be successful in bottle feeding her initially. See if your partner, or a friend, will try when you are out of the room
- Try, initially, to avoid putting her in her usual feeding position. That will make her expect the breast
- Warm the teat of the bottle, so it is more pliable
- Squeeze some breast milk onto her lips from the bottle
- Try offering her the breast first, then the bottle, when she is relaxed and not famished
- Offer her the bottle in a dark room, maybe when she has just awoken and, again, is relaxed
- Give her lots of cuddles and tenderness, so that she doesn't miss out on the closeness of breastfeeding
- If she won't take it from a bottle, try a cup, a beaker, a spoon.

THIS REFUSAL of the bottle can be very upsetting, and can make mothers miserable at the prospect of not only leaving their baby, but leaving them to starve because they won't take a bottle. It's worth thinking of ways around it: for example, depending on how old the baby is, you may be able to offer the milk in other forms. You can mix the milk with baby rice, or with other first foods. At least in this way you know your baby is getting her nourishment.

Sandy went back to work part time when her daughter was five months old. *'I was at work for two long days, and I would express at work at lunch time, having fed her before I left. I would offer her a bottle, a spout, a spoon, a cup and she didn't take any of them, but there was no use getting in a stew about it. The age factor had a lot to do with how I coped. If she had been two and a half months, I would have found it very difficult.'*

Kerrie also had problems with a bottle: *'I tried with a bottle when she was about four months old. She had had them when she was a tiny baby, and we thought it would be okay, but no way, not from anybody. Eventually we tried with a cup and because she was a big baby, that was okay. So I carried on feeding her morning and evening, and during the day she had formula from a cup. That way she didn't have the separation anxiety of feeding from a teat when I was at work – that was good as well. I'd do the same thing again.'*

VERY OFTEN mothers are told, 'Don't worry, your baby won't starve herself', which of course is true. But does it help to know that? Perhaps it is better to look with a more positive perspective at the issue – if you can't persuade her to take a bottle today, maybe she will tomorrow, or the day after that. And if she doesn't take it, there are alternatives. A battle at each feeding time is probably not going to help either the baby or the parent.

BREASTFEEDING AND THE WORKING MOTHER

THERE IS A school of thought that believes that whilst breastfeeding is fine, it is best kept in the home, and is incompatible with being a working mother. But another movement is growing more vocal, insisting that being a working mother is not all about denying that you have a family throughout the working day.

There are elements of breastfeeding and working that can be limiting, for example, the fact that some mothers do not feel they can admit that they are expressing at work.

Harriet: *'I worked for a firm of accountants – it was awful – I thought that I'd lose my credibility, particularly with my juniors, if they knew what I was doing.'*

Then there can be problems with the office 'uniform', as Louise found. *'The main problem of going back to work early was my waistline – I had nothing to wear, as all my pre-pregnancy clothes didn't fit me. Also, as I was expressing at lunch times, I couldn't wear a dress, as I would have had to strip off to express the milk.'*

Then there are the dreaded leakages, but there are ways around this, as Alex, who went back to work after her second baby was 14 weeks old, knows. *'To prevent leaks from showing, I would always make sure I had a cardigan or jacket close by. Also I treated myself to some nice bras, so I wouldn't feel so milky. I bought some camisole tops, so that you couldn't see my feeding bras through a blouse.'*

Good quality breast pads can make you feel more secure about leaks.

ALEX HIRED a pump for four months, using it daily, and her baby refused the bottle every time. She hid the milk in her food, and her baby would take juice out of a bottle. In the end she tried a formula milk that her baby took to, and the breastfeeding came to a natural end.

It is also perhaps worth investing in duplicate shirts, keeping one set at the office in case of bad leakages. Stains show less on dark and patterned materials. A spare box of breast pads in the office would be useful too.

If you aren't expressing during the day, or if you are delayed for some reason, you can get uncomfortably full. Sally is in the medical profession: *'When I first went back to work, I found that I was leaking through my operation suit, but my body adapted in a week or so. My colleagues were very supportive, and I had my own office where I could express, but if I had a late operations list, followed by a clinic, then the pressure would build up.'*

Sometimes when women return to work, their clothes change, their hair changes, maybe they start to wear perfume again. This sort of thing can have an impact on the baby. However, Louise suggests that *'you should put perfume on as soon as you have your baby, or once you get back to work and start wearing it again, your baby may react to it and refuse the breast. It also makes you feel better.'*

THESE ARE the sort of practical considerations you may think about. There are other issues that you may want to consider:

- Do you want to express at work or just feed when at home?
- How long will it take you to express in the office?
- Does your office have a room where you can express in privacy?
- Will time spent expressing be out of your lunch hour, or extra?
- Do you want anybody to know, and how will you feel if they do know?

LOOK OUT FOR:

- Engorged breasts, whilst adjusting to new feeding regime
- Blocked ducts, when commuting, cramped in one position, or when sitting in one position
- Mastitis, which can be an inflammation or infection of the breast, often caused when blocked ducts or engorgement are not remedied. This can make you feel terrible, with flu-like symptoms.

SOLUTIONS

Solutions for these problems can be any of the following:

- Don't drop feeds too quickly, or you may become engorged
- If you do feel uncomfortably full at work, express a little milk until you are comfortable
- Try not to lock your body in one position at work. See if you can remember to walk around the office every half hour or so
- If you do get engorged, make yourself as comfortable as possible in the office, and go home to a long feed from the baby, and a long bath where you can express away into the bath
- Make sure all your bras fit well
- Look after yourself. Try to keep up your energy levels with frequent, nutritious snacks and rest as much as possible in the evenings.

PROBLEMS WITH BREASTFEEDING AND WORKING

MOST PROBLEMS come about because the milk is not emptying out of the breast properly, often because the positioning is poor, and the baby isn't removing the milk as effectively as she should.

There are other factors about working that can make you more susceptible to problems.

There can be little more galling than getting a dose of mastitis as you set out to become a working mother. It is worth thinking as much as possible about how much you are doing, and how much rest you can get. Eating well, trying to avoid the office diet of coffee every half hour, moving around frequently, will all help you to keep up your supply of milk and make you work more efficiently too.

It is more effort to carry on breastfeeding when you are back at work, but there can be a tremendous sense of satisfaction if you want to do it.

WORTH THE EXTRA EFFORT

BREASTFEEDING MOTHERS who return to work often find the continuation of feeding to be a good thing. They are getting the personal fulfilment of being at work and being a wage earner, whilst they continue to maximise the nutritional benefits for their babies. Also, the baby will continue to receive antibodies through the breastmilk which will help to protect her against illness.

Sarah went back to work when her baby was three months old. *'Although I was ready to start working again, I felt Marisa could still benefit from breastfeeding. Since I was able to express milk at work, this satisfied all our requirements. There was the interest of work for me, and the knowledge that she was getting the best food. It took some organising and time but I'm glad I did it, and once I got the hang of expressing milk, the whole process got very quick and easy. I definitely think it's worth making the extra effort, particularly if you are going back when your baby is quite young.'*

Conclusion

FINDING THE BALANCE

'A BALANCING ACT', 'A juggling act', 'Never any time to yourself'. These comments are commonplace in the world of working parents. It can be quite a challenge to resolve all the needs within the family and also to participate in a satisfying role in the workplace.

On the other hand, working can give you a completeness, a sense of purpose, that you may not get without it. For many parents, raising children is their *raison d'être* at a particular stage in their lives: '*I feel I have the best of both worlds in my life at the moment. I love my children, and being with them, but that isn't the same as loving being sole carer for twelve to thirteen hours a day. Having a job to go to means I can do something for myself and then return home, happy and not at the end of my tether by tea-time. I think that these days, full-time mothering can be very isolating, and for me it's important to concentrate on more than just my children, partly because I hope it will make me more interesting to them, and also because I want them to have a female role model who works as well as cares for them.*'

If you are thinking of returning to work, it's important to find the balance that is right for you. Your life can be enriched by committing yourself to work that is within your own boundaries and limitations. This may be a couple of hours a week, or full time. Finding out what will suit you is an essential part of the process, as is looking at the different options that are available to you. Everybody is different, and what suits one person can be anathema to another. Whilst you cannot pretend that there is only you to please after having a family, it's also important to remember to put yourself high on the list of priorities. Think about what is important to you, and then see how this can be incorporated within the needs of others in your life.

This is a good time to be considering the variety of workstyles that are available. With part time, full time and flexitime as options, plus working from home made possible by the advent of technology, you can examine the choices in the knowledge that there is far less emphasis on the 'all or nothing' approach. Women are likely to continue to want children, but are not so easily replaceable at work, as their levels of responsibility and status have risen to a greater extent than ever before. This means that more employers will be prepared to listen to you and put the needs of working parents higher on their agenda.

As Laura says: *'It's all about balance. If you can get it right, you can look forward to a very fulfilling lifestyle, enriched by what is important to you.'*

Directory

THIS CONTAINS the names and addresses of useful organisations, and a little bit more besides, like the essence of the organisation, or relevant quotes from their literature, to give you a better idea of their purpose.

HOME RUN
Active Information,
Cribau Mill, Llanvair Discoed,
Chepstow, Gwent NP6 6RD
01291 641222
'This monthly magazine for professional homeworkers has more than 1,000 subscriptions...'
Articles in the May 1995 edition include:
- Virtual teamwork: how two heads can create more business
- Effective design: why looks can be more important than words
- Case study: how planning changed a 'softie' into a business woman
- PR: how to write the perfect press release
- Presenting: straight talking: how to prepare a powerful presentation.

KIDS' CLUB NETWORK
Bellerive House, 3 Muirfield Crescent,
London E14 9SZ
0171 512 2112
This organisation is devoted to improving the quality of after school care. It offers:
- Practical help and support to those wishing to start up a Kids' Club
- Advice and information to government and local authorities on the need for more out of school clubs

- An information helpline for parents, playworkers, schools, and others
- Training for playcare workers
- A list of publications, including a regular magazine
- A consultancy service for employers to advise on childcare support.

NATIONAL CHILDCARE
CAMPAIGN/DAYCARE TRUST
4 Wild Court, London WC2B 4AU
0171 405 5617
This charity provides reports, guides and information packs such as:
- Becoming a breadwinner: policies to assist lone parents with childcare
- Childcare: the European challenge
- Under five and under funded
- ABC for providers: daycare and the Children Act 1989.

They also produce a magazine: *Childcare Now*, plus they give free information and advice about childcare and early years' services.

NCT WORKING MOTHERS' GROUPS
NCT, Alexandra House,
Oldham Terrace, Acton,
London W3 6NH
0181 992 8637
More and more branches of the National Childbirth Trust are setting up Working Mothers' Groups, and finding that often they are the most successful part of the branch, with so many parents going back to work.

This is a sample of what one group has to offer:

- Support, for women in paid employment
- A network upon which to share experiences of balancing work and home
- Practical information about local childcare options
- Support for parents trying to improve employment policies and practice.

They hold a monthly meeting, either in the evening or at weekends. Each meeting has a topic, for example: *preparing children for school; enlightening your employer; children's sleep problems; family dental care; local day care provision, family outings and a summer barbecue.*

NEW WAYS TO WORK
309 Upper Street,
London N1 2TY
0171 226 4026
This is an independent charity which *'aims to change the culture in the workplace to give real freedom of choice to individuals who cannot or do not wish to work traditional patterns'.*

The difference between this organisation and others already mentioned is that, although they work closely with Parents at Work, their brief is not related to childcare issues. Although parents are often those in need of flexible working, New Ways to Work is looking in general at this, so it can be relevant to carers of elderly people, or individuals who simply don't want to fit into the traditional mould.

They provide a range of publications, information and advice, for example, help with negotiations, they give talks and run seminars, particularly for employers and personnel departments.

PARENTS AT WORK
5th Floor, 45 Beech Street,
Barbican, London, EC2Y 8AD
0171 628 3578
First of all, they publish books and guides for both employers and working parents.

Their list of publications includes: *Balancing Work and Home; Employer's Guide to Childcare; Returners' Guide; Working Parents' Handbook* (which is a guide to alternatives in childcare and factors in making a choice).

They also run workshops and their training programmes include: *Going on maternity leave; preparing to return to the workplace; preparing fathers for fatherhood; maternity pay and policy; flexible working policies; the family friendly agenda in the workplace.*

With membership, you receive a copy of the *Working Parents' Handbook*, a regular magazine, and the option of meeting up with local groups. Some local groups are run as joint Parents at Work/NCT Working Mothers' Groups.

What one company has done through Parents at Work
Louisa is employed by Parents at Work (PAW) as a Childcare Development/Information Officer in a large multinational.

'The purpose of this service was to give an unbiased, high quality information service to company employees. When the company made it clear they wanted to do this, PAW put in a tender and won.

We have a broad brief: our service is available to everyone who works in the company, whether male or female. It gives people options, informed choice, up to date research on existing facilities, such as nurseries.

We run in-house workshops on returning to work and maternity leave. We produce information sheets, and a newsletter three times a year. This all stems from the realisation that the welfare of the family impacts upon the worker, so we aim to support the working parent as much as possible, short of choosing the childcare, of course.

This company offers family-friendly policies, with options of flexitime, part-time, job sharing, term-time working, homeworking, but it also recognises the possible problem issues connected with these policies, such as isolation, lack of continuity and poor communication, perception of role from colleagues.'

THE MATERNITY ALLIANCE
45 Beech Street, Barbican,
London EC2Y 8AD
0171 588 8582

To quote its mission statement:
'The Maternity Alliance is an independent national organisation which campaigns for improvements in rights and services for mothers, fathers and babies. It works for better provision before conception, and during pregnancy, childbirth and the first year of life.'

The Maternity Alliance runs training days on maternity rights with the Trades Union Congress and also runs its own courses.

They carry out research and organise seminars on key maternity issues, and they publish leaflets. Send an SAE for leaflets on maternity rights and benefits, and reports, such as the *'Maternity Alliance Disability Working Group Pack'*, and *'Women, Work and Maternity: Women's Experiences of Working During Pregnancy, of Maternity Leave and the Return to Work'*.

UNIONS

IF YOUR company is unionised, you can make use of this to ensure you get fair treatment, as an employee, as a woman, and as a parent. Unions will offer support in negotiating for childcare assistance, or career breaks and job shares. If you have a union you may well find that policies are already in place, but representatives will generally be supportive in helping you get the best deal.

For example, a career break structure introduced by one union, represents good practice. The basic points of this discretionary scheme are:

- It is open to both men and women, who can apply and reach a decision before starting a family
- Two periods of leave are possible, for a maximum of two years each, which can be full or part time
- Employee's and employer's contributions to the pension scheme can be maintained
- Flexibility or part-time return is possible
- Return to same grade at same or nearby location is provided.

WOMEN RETURNERS' NETWORK
8 John Adam Street, London WC2N 6EZ
0171 839 8188

'Ten years ago, Ruth Michaels, Director of Continuing Education at Hatfield Polytechnic, realised that, although many organisations around the country were working closely with women returners, each was doing so in isolation to the others. Knowing well the advantages of sharing ideas, good practice and effort, she got together a group of her contacts . . . and so the Women's Returners' Network was born.

Activities now include research, projects with employers, conferences and seminars, the development and dissemination of model training programmes such as Professional Updating for Women, building up expertise in obtaining European money from schemes such as New Opportunities for Women (NOW) and of course providing advice and assistance to individual women returners.'
[*Return: newsletter of WRN*, December 1994, no 16]

One of their major publications is *Returning to Work: A Directory of Education and Training for Women*. This includes details of:
- What to look for in a course
- Whether childcare facilities are available
- Costs and possible sponsors
- Women's training centres and support groups nationally.

WORKING FOR CHILDCARE
77 Holloway Road, London N7 8JZ
0171 700 0281

Working for Childcare describes itself as a national voluntary organisation whose main aim is to promote high quality affordable childcare for all working parents who need it. This includes the low paid, shift workers, part-timers, home workers and those on training courses. They promote the development of affordable quality childcare through encouraging parents, employers, trades unions, trainers, local councils and the government to work together. They provide practical advice and information through:

- Their telephone advice line
- A bimonthly newsletter
- Regular publications and research documents
- Regular conference and training programmes
- They also run a specialist childcare consultancy service.

OTHER USEFUL ADDRESSES

British Activity Holiday Association
22 Green Lane, Hersham,
Walton on Thames KT12 5HD
01932 252994

This organisation was formed by activity centre operators in 1986. Its intention was to establish operating guidelines, such as a Code of Practice and Inspection Scheme, for activity centres where previously there were none.

CACHE (Council for Awards in Children's Care and Education)
8 Chequer Street, St Albans, Herts,
AL1 3XZ
01727 847 636

Employers for Childcare
0171 233 0355

Gingerbread
49 Wellington Street
London WC2E 7BN
0171 336 8184

Support network for single parents.

Home Office
Immigration Department
Lunar House, 40 Wellesley Road,
Croydon CR9 2BY
0181 686 0688
or 0181 760 1666 for recorded information

For information on regulations about au pairs.

National Childminding Association
8 Masons Hill, Bromley, Kent BR2 9EY
0181 466 0200

Information resources for minders and parents.

National Council for One Parent Families
255 Kentish Town Rd
London NW5 2LX
0171 267 1361

Advice and support for single parents returning to work. Running Department of Employment backed schemes.

Pre-school Learning Alliance
69 King's Cross Road
London WC1X 9LL
0171 833 0991

National educational charity, which through its member pre-schools is the largest single provider of education and care for children under five.

National Early Years Network
77 Holloway Road
London N7 8JZ
0171 607 9573

Further reading

All Party Parliamentary Group on Parenting and
International Year of the Family 1995: UK.
Report of the Parliamentary Hearing

Charlotte Breese and Hilary Gomer 1993:
Good Nanny Guide. Vermilion.

Jenny Hewison and Therese Dowswell 1994:
Child Health Care and the Working Mother - The
Juggling Act. Chapman Hall.

Adrienne Katz 1992: The Juggling Act.
Bloomsbury.

Gayle Kimball 1988: 50/50 Parenting.
Lexington Books.

Frankie McGowan 1994: Women Going Back to
Work. N & P.

Hilli Matthews 1995: Au Pairs Without Tears.
Problems Unlimited Agency, Windsor.

1995: Returning to Work - A Guide For Lone
Parents. National Council for One Parent
Families.

1994: Balancing Work and Home. Parents at
Work.

Revised 1994: Working Parents' Handbook.
Parents at Work.

Lee Rodwell and Mary Tidyman 1995:
Working Parents' Survival Handbook. Health
Education Authority.

Index

after-school play schemes 138-9
agencies, childcare 68-9
  and au pairs 129
  and nannies 113, 129
allocating tasks 49-51
assertiveness skills 42-3
au pair plus 125
au pairs 60, 61, 62, 125-9
  and abuse of hospitality 129
  advantages 126
  and babysitting 126
  and car insurance 127
  compared with nannies 128
  cost 125, 126
  disadvantages 127
  and emergencies 129
  finding 129
  and housework 63, 125
  and privacy 129
  responsibility for 127
  and trust 129

babies
  and childminders 81, 82
  leaving with carer 32-3
  in nurseries 96-8
  and nursery places 92
  and separation anxiety 32, 40-1
  and tiredness 34-5
  see also breastfeeding
babysitters 53, 55
  au pairs as 126
  and choice of childcare 66-8

nannies as 103
balancing work and home 31-45, 170-1
  part-time work 36-9
  and responsibility for childcare 44-5
  separation from the baby 32-3
  and sick children 39-40
  telephoning carers 33
  and tiredness 34-5
bottle-feeding 162, 163-6
breastfeeding 145-69
  breast pads 167
  expressing milk 151, 152-62
    by hand 154, 157-9
    pumps for 154-5, 159-61
    at work 163, 168, 169
    see also expressed breast milk (EBM)
  flexibility of 153
  how it works 148-50
  leakages 167
  let down reflex 149-50, 156-7, 159, 164
  maintaining the bond 147
  and mastitis 168, 169
  NCT breastfeeding counsellors 150
  night-time feeding 151-2
  positioning the baby 150, 151
  and proximity to office 62
  reasons to continue 147-8
  and relaxation 148

and returning to work 145-6, 166-9
  and shared parenthood 48
  at start of day 147
  see also expressed breast milk (EBM)
British Activity Holiday Association 143

Camp Beaumont 143
career breaks 15
  and pensions 6
  and updating work skills 7
career changes 13-14, 51-2
cars
  access to, and choice of childcare 64-5
  and au pairs 127
  and nannies 102
changing needs 131-7
childcare 59-71
  agencies 68-9, 129
  availability of 60
  changing arrangements 65-6
  choices 60-5
    and access to a car 64-5
    finding local carers 64-5
  contracts of employment 70-1, 87
  costs of 61, 62
  and domestic help 63
  initial thoughts about 59-60
  interviewing carers 69-70
  organising 31-2
  and proximity to office/home 62

selecting carers 68-9
and separation anxiety 40-1
sharing responsibility for
44-5, 47-51
childhood influences, and
returning to work 9
childminders 31-2, 60-1, 73-
87
accountability of 77
advantages of 74-7
after-school 137-8
changing 80-1, 86
and children at school 63
children settling with 84
children's view of 87
choosing 70
costs of 61, 76
disadvantages of 77-81
and discipline 83
expertise of 76-7
as extended family 74, 86
finding 65, 66, 87
and first-time mothers 76-7,
86
and flexibility 75-6
and food 84
local authority inspections
73
as mother figures 74, 81
and older children 77
and other children 78-9
and personality clashes 78-9
pre-registration courses 73
reasons for becoming 81-2
registered 65, 71, 73
relationships with 79-81
and sickness 78
and smacking 84
and transition to nurseries
95-6
and unconventional work-
ing hours 75
Children Act (1989) 135
and childminders 74, 77

and nurseries 90-1, 99
and play schemes 143
contracts with carers 70-1, 87
nannies 118-21
crèches *see* nurseries; workplace crèches

daily routine
establishing 31-2, 41
and live-in nannies 102-3
divorce, and future security 6
domestic help 63

EBM *see* expressed breast
milk
electric breast pumps 160-1
emergencies, and au pairs 129
evening work, and childcare
63
expressed breast milk (EBM)
bottled 163-6
and choice of childcare 67,
68
defrosting 162
freezing 154, 161-2
office conditions 163
storing 162, 163
transporting 163
see also breastfeeding

family activities 55-7
family life 47-57
partnership pressures 52-3
shared parenting 47-51
sharing responsibilities with
other families 56
unexpected events 51
family-friendly jobs 12
fathers *see* male partners
feelings
talking about 21-9
see also guilt
first-time mothers, and childminders 76-7, 86

flexible working 12-13
flexitime 17
food, and childminders 84
friends
children's school friends 140
informal childcare by 132-3
full-time motherhood, and
feelings of isolation 21, 26
full-time work
and choice of childcare 63
percentage of mothers in 12
personal experiences of 25,
27-8
returning to 13

Gingerbread 54
grandparents
informal childcare by 134-7
and school holidays 140
guilt
and breastfeeding 146
and childcare choices 70-1
and returning to work 1-2,
34
and taking time off 57

holidays
annual holidays 140
school holidays 139-43
housework, and au pairs 63,
125
husbands *see* male partners

illness, balancing work and
home 39-40
informal childcare 131-7
friends and acquaintances
132-3
neighbours 132
relatives 134-7
International Year of the
Family 1994 12
isolation, and full-time motherhood 3, 21, 26

Kids' Club Network (KCN) 139

lifestyles, returning to work 12-19

male partners
  death of 6
  and part-time working 37-8, 44
  redundancy 8, 26, 51
  relationships with 52-4
  and shared parenthood 48-51
  sharing responsibility for childcare 44-5
  spending time with 53-4
Maternity Alliance 2
Maternity Allowance 2
maternity leave 2
  negotiating 41-2
maternity nurses 123
maternity pay (SMP) 2
maternity rights 2
men *see* male partners
mother's helps 61-2, 124

nannies 9, 61, 101-21
  and abuse of hospitality 105
  age of 103-4
  application questions 114
  and babysitting 103
  building relationships with 71
  compared with au pairs 128
  contracts of employment 118-21
  cost 61, 62, 102, 103, 106
  daily 107-8
  and fast turnover 106
  finding 66, 113
  and housework 63, 104, 107
  interviewing

by telephone 113-15
  face to face 115-18
  and living space 107
  living-in 101, 102-7
    advantages of 102-5
    disadvantages of 105-7
  personal experiences of 108-10
  personality clashes with 105
  references 118
  relationships with children 104-5
  sharing 110-13
  and time-saving ideas 56
  trusting 106, 107
  use of car 102
NCT (National Childbirth Trust)
  breastfeeding counsellors 150
  groups 3, 4
negotiating returning to work 41-2
neighbours, informal child care by 132
nurseries 61, 89-99
  accountability 90-1
  advantages of 89-91
  booking places 92
  as child-centred 89
  children adjusting to 96
  children settling in 94
  choosing 93-6, 98-9
  and competition 92
  costs 92
  disadvantages 92-3
  as extended families 94
  finding 66, 99
  inspection and registration 90
  nursery nurses' views 96-8
  opening hours 90, 92
  and other children 90
  parents dropping in to 90

and quality control 91
  registered 71
  state-run 62
  telephoning 33
  and variety of carers 91
  workplace 13
  workplace crèches 13, 61, 62, 89, 94-5
nursery classes, in private schools 91

older children 131-43
  and childminders 77, 131

parental responsibility, for older children 133
part-time work 12, 15-16
  balancing work and home 36-9
  by male partners 37-8, 44
  and choice of childcare 63
partners *see* male partners
pensions, and career breaks 6
personal experiences 21-9
play schemes
  after-school 138
  school holidays 140-3
postnatal depression, personal experiences of 21, 25
privacy
  and au pairs 129
  and nannies 105
private play schemes 140-3
private schools, 'prep' time 139

redundancy, of male partners 8, 26, 51
relatives, informal childcare by 134-7
returning to work 1-19
  and breastfeeding 145-6, 166-9
  and guilt 1-2, 34

lifestyles 12-19
maternity rights 2
negotiating 41-2
reasons for 3-12
role models, and shared
    parenthood 48, 49
role reversal 19

school days 137-43
    after-school childminders
        137-8
    after-school play schemes
        138-9
school holidays 139-43
self-employment 17-18
separation anxiety 32, 40-1
shared parenting 47-51
    allocating tasks 49-51
sick children 39-40

single parenthood
    balancing work and home
        45
    and evening work 63
    personal experiences of 22-4
    and returning to work 10-
        11
    and support 54-5
smacking, and childminders
    84
statutory maternity leave 2
statutory maternity pay
    (SMP) 2
Superwoman, idea of 8
Sweden, maternity rights 2

time
    spent with partners 53-4
    time-saving ideas 56

tiredness 34-5
toddlers 131
transport, and choice of
    childcare 64-5

unconventional working
    hours, and childminders 75
unexpected events, redundan-
    cies 51

working from home 16-17
    and breastfeeding 146
    and choice of childcare 63
working life, changes after
    parenthood 31-2
workplace crèches 13, 61, 62,
    89, 94-5